Mihir Vatsa (b. 1991) is a riverwalker from Hazaribagh, Jharkhand. He is a widely-published poet with awards from the Charles Wallace India Trust, Srinivas Rayaprol Poetry Prize and Toto Funds the Arts, Bangalore. Mihir studied English Literature at Ramjas College, University of Delhi, and is presently a PhD candidate at the Indian Institute of Technology, Delhi. He can be reached on his Instagram @tales.of.hazaribagh.

Praise for *Tales of Hazaribagh*

'This book is like Hazaribagh—it has a gentle gravity that keeps us with it as sleep does to dreams. Written to the speed of discovery, it moves gracefully through history, between the archive and experience, to leave us with a landscape that we will, from now on, remember like we do our bed.'

—Sumana Roy

'Mihir Vatsa's book, *Tales of Hazaribagh*, elicited quite a number of responses from me. I was surprised: for I did not know that there was an emu farm in Jharkhand! I admired the author's craft: for it is more than just a memoir or a travelogue. There is philosophy, there are personal experiences (including a spine-chilling story), there is an account of how the history, politics, and people of a place shape that place. It made me envious: for there is so much to be written about Jharkhand and there are several ideas bubbling inside my own head, but I have no idea if I could ever be as observant, patient, and accomplished like Vatsa to write all of it down. In Vatsa's prose, there are three components that are vital for writing about a place and its people: love, earnestness, and humility. This is a book that will be remembered.'

—Hansda Sowvendra Shekhar

TALES *of* HAZARIBAGH

An Intimate Exploration of Chhotanagpur Plateau

Mihir Vatsa

SPEAKING TIGER

SPEAKING TIGER BOOKS LLP
125A, Ground Floor, Shahpur Jat, near Asiad Village,
New Delhi 110049

Published by Speaking Tiger Books in paperback 2021

ISBN: 978-93-5447-038-7
eISBN: 978-93-5447-039-4

10 9 8 7 6 5 4 3 2 1

Typeset in Electra LT Std by SÜRYA, New Delhi
Printed at …

Like lovestruck,

&

for the land

‘I don’t mean the town itself, of course, but the country which surrounds it.’

—Edward Abbey, *Desert Solitaire*

Contents

NORTH

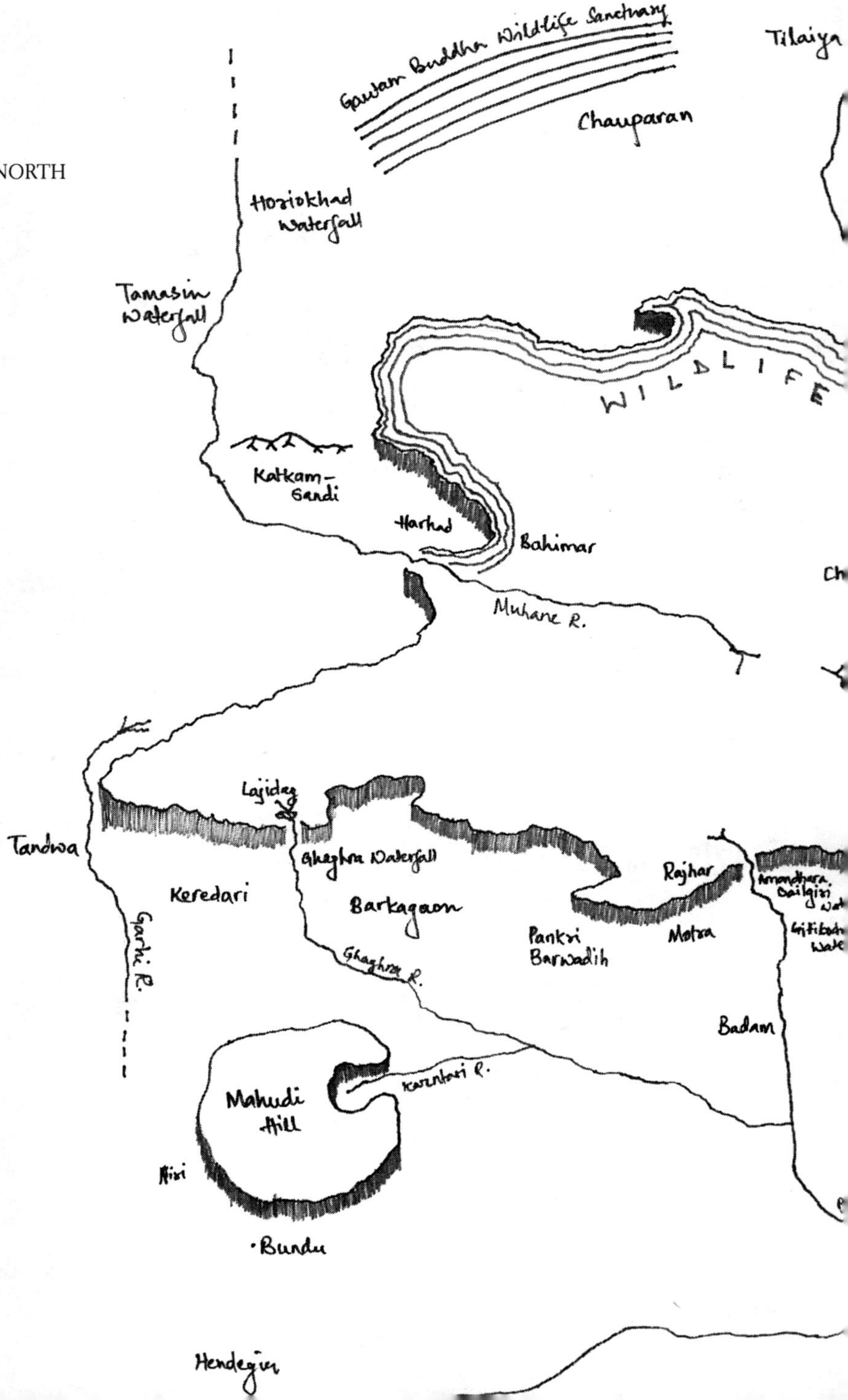

Gautam Buddha Wildlife Sanctuary
Tilaiya
Chauparan
Horiokhad Waterfall
Tamasin Waterfall
WILDLIFE
Katkam-Sandi
Harhad
Bahimar
Muhane R.
Lajidag
Tandwa
Ghaghra Waterfall
Keredari
Barkagaon
Rajhar
Pankri Barwadih
Motra
Garhi R.
Ghaghra R.
Badam
Karnari R.
Mahudi Hill
Bundu
Hendegir

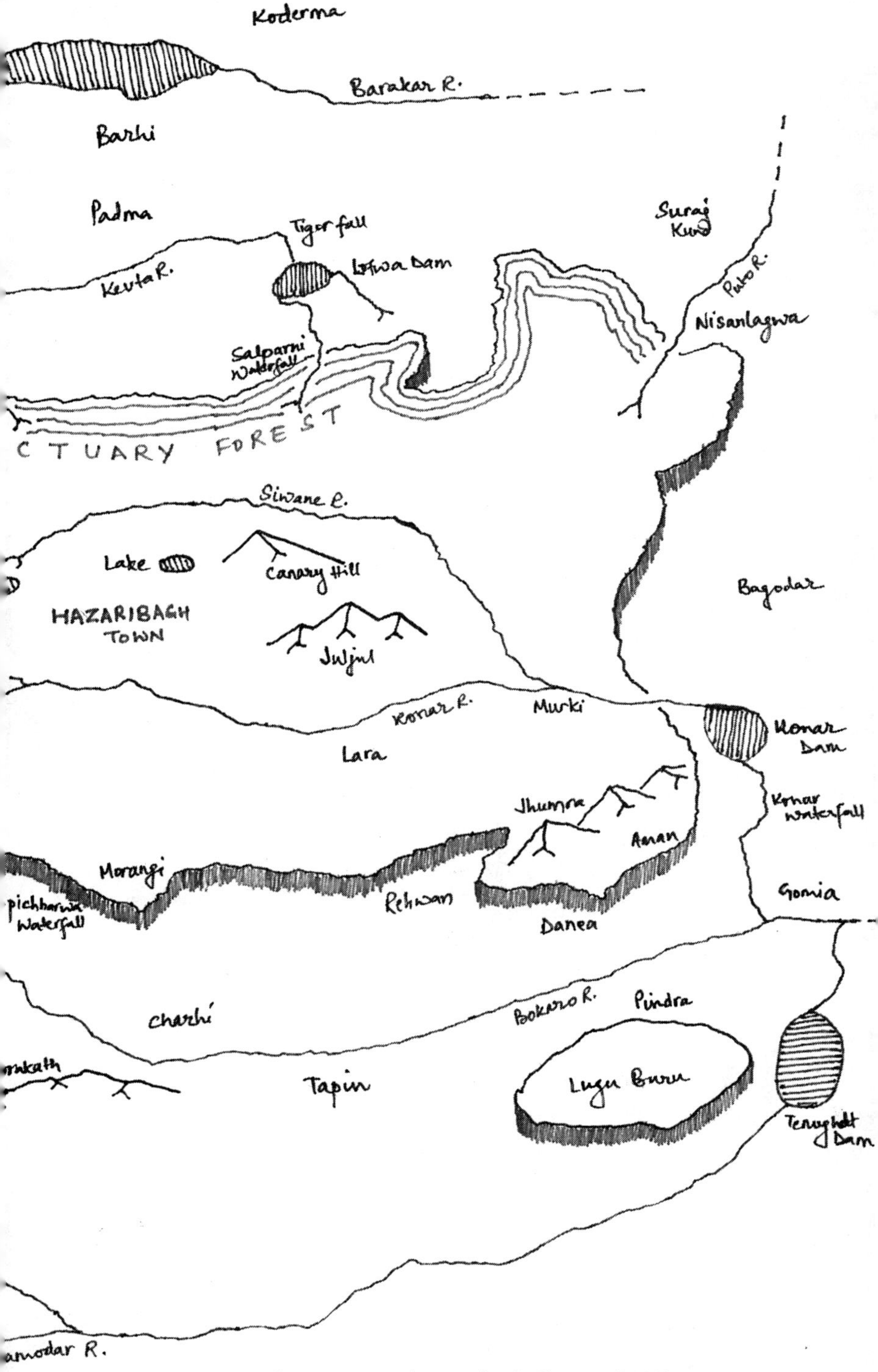

Indicative map of Hazaribagh Plateau (2021)

Sanatorium

I remember it was not particularly sunny that day.

I woke up in time to reach the office by ten. I had got no sleep the night before—or the one before that.

It was September, the year 2016. Delhi had turned grey, and Adhchini, the village where I lived, greyer. There was one main alley that cut through the village. The ground was narrow and everything above it was dark. In the day, the place would be heavy with soot rising from snacks stalls and settling on the wires overhead. It was a quintessential Delhi village where I lived in a small 1BHK.

I checked the time on the phone, took out my umbrella and locked the door. Climbing down the stairs, I emerged at the food stall that sent me dinner every night. I nodded at the owner, Love Bhaiya, both of us flashing smiles at each other, and walked out of the alley.

My office was a small ad agency, tucked secretively in the bustling Hauz Khas Village. I was a copywriter.

I had quietly followed in the footsteps of Kriti, my senior in college by a year, to become her junior at the agency too. The previous year in August, I had come to Delhi from Hazaribagh to meet my friends from college. I learned from

Kriti then that she had to leave for Mumbai for a new project, and that the company was looking for a replacement. I was uncertain, non-committal.

A week later, as I was still in Delhi, Kriti called early in the morning, asking if I could meet her in an hour.

'Baba, *naukri chahiye*? See me at the station—bye!'

Baba put his initial hesitation aside and agreed. Baba thought that it would be an 'interesting experience'.

In the metro, she taught me some basics of advertising. ATL, BTL: Above the Line, Below the Line. SKU was Stock Keeping Unit. She did mostly BTL work at the agency.

'It is fun—something that needs to be appreciated more,' she said.

My very informal interview happened inside the office's kitchen. Five minutes later, I was an employee being briefed for the day.

On my way to work that September morning in the auto, I remembered it all.

The sequence: first job, first day, first colleagues, first clients. I had completed an eventful year—I never thought I would be an adman. When I was a child, the ambition, of course, was to be an IAS officer. Then it turned into becoming an aeronautical engineer. Then a fashion designer, then a writer, then an academic. Advertising was nowhere in the chart.

But it had been a good year: being creative, spontaneous, putting educational training to industrial use.

I got down from the auto at Sahoday Vidyalaya and opted to walk the remaining course. On this stretch, the road ascends higher with the ground and the sharp boundaries of Deer Park forest on either side turn it into an earthly avenue. Such places are a small consolation in Delhi.

Yet, the city made itself visible through autos plying on the road, the long sedans honking at other long sedans, and garbage that lay rotting in a corner. This pile of rubbish always seemed to increase, if not in volume then in stench. Some yards ahead, the kiosks lined up steadily to the right. There was a large public parking by the village entrance. Inside, however, it was *parking for villagers only*.

I found this sign amusing because from what I had seen of villagers back home, they were often poor. I was from Jharkhand, and in Jharkhand, not many villagers owned cars. Smiling, I called for tea at the stall. The tea from this stall was good. It started our days. The tea we made in office was something else. The concoction couldn't start anything, let alone our days.

At lunch hour, I went up to Kriti at her desk.

She had been in Mumbai about three months, but in the end, she found Delhi better. After she returned, the agency retained us both.

When it was just the two of us in the hall, I told her about my appointment with the psychologist.

'You did the right thing,' she said, 'It was about time—you need to take care of yourself.'

In college, Kriti and I had bonded over our love for writing.

We were both poets, we were both in the literary society, and we were both Aquarians. Whenever logic failed, we rationalized life through astrology. Over the years, we came to regard each other as long-lost 'Kumbh' siblings. I knew some of her secrets and she knew some of mine. There was an element of carefree, childish trust that we had fostered between us. Nothing was too shocking or scandalous for either her or me, and though we did not really lead scandalous lives, I still hesitated talking with her about my depression, because the matter was so confusing and personal.

After work, I walked slowly to the clinic at Green Park. The grotto was located deep in the basement of a building. I took the stairs down to the reception and waited. I had booked my appointment through an app the night before and was unsure if the digital process would work. It did. Fifteen minutes later, the doctor saw me.

'Tell me about yourself, Mihir *ji*,' he adjusted his posture in the chair, his eyes fixed attentively on me.

'Well… I come from this town called Hazaribagh in Jharkhand,' I began, arranging words in my mind, one sentence after the other, a chain of thoughts, a train starting on the tracks.

Around two centuries before my birth, in 1764, the East India Company obtained the diwani rights of Bengal after winning the battles of Plassey and Buxar. Consequently, the huge forest tract of the Chhotanagpur came under the Company's rule.

At that time, the Grand Trunk Road which ran east-west along the Chhotanagpur Plateau was dilapidated and without bridges. This road was notorious for theft and dacoities. Its reputation terrorized travellers, discouraging them from entering the jungle that extended beyond it.

Quite aptly, the region was dubbed the 'Junglebury district' by the British. It was a mysterious province of many myths, this Chhotanagpur, home to sneaky tigers, exotic rituals, and primitive tribes. Here, the tigers were more cunning.

I grew up hearing many stories of these tigers. In one of the stories that I remember which goes back to '*angrezon ke samay mein*', to the colonial period, the tigers would wait quietly for the *push-push* bearers who ferried travellers from one place to the other in a palanquin-like contraption. At dusk, instead of attacking the men, the tigers would steal a terrifying glimpse from them. The sight of a tiger would lead the bearers to abandon the contraption in a hurry, leaving the poor passenger unguarded inside.

This was the Grand Trunk Road of the late eighteenth century, before it was repaired, before the bridges came up. On its northern side stood the Parasnath Mountain, the highest landmass of the plateau and also its end, which was a revered landmark for Jains. I would see this mountain from the windows of state transport buses whenever I travelled to Hazaribagh from Dhanbad. Some distance ahead and on the left appeared a long, loose landmass that looked like hills. Very few outsiders had travelled beyond this escarpment. The forest was considered impenetrable, and it often was.

The British colonizers may have defeated armies and they may have reduced several Rajas to their subjects, but they could not defeat the tropical climate of the Gangetic

Plains. Away from their temperate homes in Britain, the companymen in Calcutta were keen to escape from a climate that was not hospitable to them.

Sometime in the 1770s, the British waded through one of the forest passages of the Chhotanagpur, following an ancient pilgrim route, the Old Benaras Road,[1] and arrived on top of a plateau. This was the plateau of Hazaribagh, my hometown. It was a highland that exists within the larger Chhotanagpur, extending roughly fifty kilometres along the east-west and forty kilometres along the north-south axes. On the plateau, they found villages: Mukundganj, Okni, Kolghatti.

That the British arrived late to the region does not mean that the plateau itself was uninhabited. Humans had lived here since prehistoric times, and when the companymen came, the present-day Hazaribagh was under the zamindari of Ramgarh Raj. It was Captain Camac from Calcutta who engineered the Raja's compliance, and soon the company became the de-facto ruler of the plateau. A military battalion named after the zamindari estate was raised, and it was stationed, probably, near the village of Okni.

As the battalion rooted itself to the land, facilities like shops and weekly markets, residential constructions like administrators' bungalows, and military constructions like the cantonment, gradually shaped the table-top into a station. This station, in the 1786 map of Major James Rennell, appeared as Ocunhazary, and by 1813, it had graduated into a town.[2]

This small town, located at a humble 600 metres above sea level and boasting an excellent climate, soon came to be known as Hazaribagh, the land of a thousand gardens, the land of a thousand tigers.

The station of Hazaribagh was compared often with two more stations of the East India Company. The first was Darjeeling, the other at Jabalpur.

Hazaribagh was located, altitude-wise, between the two. It wasn't too high and it wasn't too low. Both the deciduous sal and the coniferous pine could grow on the plateau, the latter albeit with some effort. The administrators' bungalows had their own huge gardens and the streets were shaded under a canopy of trees.[3] Proper avenues were built, shadows of which linger along the present Hirabag to DVC Chowk Road, the Forest Colony Road, the SP Kothi to Kunwar Singh Chowk Road, the roads of Julu Park, portions of Lake Road, and others.

There are very few books written about the colonial history of Hazaribagh, but the handful that exist never forget to mention the picturesque landscape and the 'salubrity' of its climate. Tall sal trees, pastoral wilderness, idyllic retreat—Hazaribagh was increasingly being identified through these references. Hazaribagh's attraction among the British gained attention of two amateur artists with the company: Captain Robert Smith, who visited the town in 1813, and the more famous Sir Charles D'Oyly, who visited the plateau a decade later in 1823. Their sketches remain the earliest visual documentation of Hazaribagh's landscape.

The word 'salubrity' was first used for the town by one G. Hunter Thompson in his geographical survey report.

Thompson was a surveyor with the British Raj and was

evidently charmed by the place. He visited Hazaribagh twice, first in 1858–59 and later in 1862–63. The 1857 Revolt was over. The Empire was real. Thompson's experience with Hazaribagh had made him privy to the conditions of the soldiers at the station. The place impressed him, and he wrote in his report that it had become a tradition to send ailing soldiers from the plains to recuperate up in the plateau.

The men came to improve their health for battles that lay ahead of them. It wouldn't be out of place to suggest that soldiers were the first tourists in Hazaribagh. Thompson wrote that after the men were healthy again and when it was time to leave, they left 'in excellent health and with many regrets.' Thompson's attraction towards the place was so strong that he even recommended Hazaribagh as an option for the new capital of India.[4]

One of my favourite things to do when I lived in Delhi as a student and later as an advertising professional was to look up Hazaribagh on Google. While many of my old friends were happy to have made the transition from a small town to their respective cities where they studied, I, on the other hand, would miss the forest, the landscape and the climate of Hazaribagh. By the time I completed my BA, my classmates and friends in the hostel knew two things: I was from Hazaribagh, and that it was a beautiful place. I just wouldn't stop talking about it!

Spurred by homesickness, I spent hours looking for news, literature, blogs or old photos of Hazaribagh on the internet. During those searches, I found a lot of material on the town's local history. Thompson's geographical survey report, PC Roy Choudhury's excellent collection of facts, trivia and official correspondence letters in *Hazaribagh Old Records*, Rabindranath Tagore's short memoir of travelling to Hazaribagh 'Ten Days Holiday', the sketches of Robert Smith and Sir Charles D'Oyly—among many others.

Reading these accounts and stories, particularly Roy Choudhury's *Hazaribagh Old Records*, I understood how Hazaribagh, initially a 'military station', soon turned into a 'hill station'. I also realized how the poetic outlook towards the place, cultivated after the arrival of Bengali settlers, created a new imagination for the town. Besides, this shift was aided by the cultural perception that all high places that offered a climate favourable to the British were hill stations.

But Hazaribagh was essentially a plateau. It was neither on top of a hill nor was it surrounded by hills. The table-top was hard, plain, often barren. It had a cluster of seven hills, none of them particularly high, and these hills too existed in their own solitude. No imposing or unifying range connected them.

'Eddies,' Scottish writer Nan Shepherd called such hills on the Cairngorms. The word is fitting for the hills of Hazaribagh too.

Did I tell all of this to the doctor?

Not really. I mean, not so much the history part. I told him things about Hazaribagh in bits.

I told him about myself, how Hazaribagh had instilled in me an appreciation for nature, how the place made me write about it in my poems.

'I have won awards too, writing poems about Hazaribagh,' I said. I told him how my first poetry collection, in which Hazaribagh figures heavily, led me to a prestigious writing fellowship in the UK.

I told him about a waterfall that I had found in the forest and also about my wish to return someday. Idealism. I said, 'I want to *do something* for the town'.

It is only now that I understand that you don't always need to *do something* for the town. That it can also do *things* to you.

'You should come and see Hazaribagh someday,' I extended an invitation. 'Our home is by a lake.'

He smiled and took notes.

The quiet in the room, in the space between us, grew heavy.

I looked for a window, but realized we were in the basement after all. The lone ventilator higher up on the wall showed the cloudy sky outside.

'Mihir *ji*, why are you in Delhi?'

The precision in his question caught me off-guard.

'I have a job here,' I said. He nodded.

'You said you were a poet, didn't you? That writing makes you happy.'

I did indeed say that.

'Are you sure you are fit for this, this... *grind*, as you put it yourself? Do you still write?'

I wanted to be fit for my job. I was more than a poet.

Besides, people don't introduce themselves as poets anymore, do they? I was twenty-five. I could handle the hours, I could do anything. Millions of twenty-five-year olds across the world were doing the same.

'Have you considered going back? Maybe take up freelance work. The internet makes things so much easier these days.'

I had imagined that after finishing my studies in Delhi, I would be back in Hazaribagh, helming an NGO or something similar. That was always the plan. But life was so swift in the capital, it didn't allow the leisure for thought.

I was often making quick decisions, acting impulsively, changing accommodation from one locality to the other, ignoring my friends, forcing myself into a deluge of work. I was experiencing for the first time what steady money does to people. It had seduced me into a routine. What I had imagined for myself was different from what I had turned into. Besides, returning to that imagination seemed self-serving, selfish, and we are taught not to be selfish.

The twenty-five-year-old Mihir saw people climbing up their careers and was convinced that it was the right way to go. No one was going the other way, after all. Who knew if the other way existed in the first place? Frost's poem is, after all, a poem in the end. It is not the annual increment.

I should clarify here that I wasn't homesick for the *people* in my hometown. Most of my friends, like me, had moved out of Hazaribagh after school. We had become visitors, catching up with the homeland during vacations or holidays.

Now, without familiar faces, the town was just a crowd. After living in Delhi and being a part of a big-city crowd for seven years, I was homesick actually for the plateau. I was missing the sal trees, the water in the lake, the wind on top of the hill. People mattered less, the land asserted more.

For all my interest in local history too, I wasn't drawn to the town either. There are always too many people and towns in India. There are never enough waterfalls.

I was hurting in Delhi, but the fledgling professional inside of me often talked me out of it. Perhaps a better salary would work. Perhaps a new workplace. So I shifted, and took up a job at an NGO in Noida.

From the previous cuboid at Adhchini, I moved into a spacious apartment. I loved that apartment. It had a full bathtub. I would only gaze at the bathtub, never filling it up, never using it, not deeming myself worthy of that luxury. There was such a sense of achievement, a bit of pride too. I was the governor of my 2BHK. *Tonight, I will put one leg in this room, one leg in the other, and my arms in the kitchen.* I was even able to save some money.

I mixed easily with my new colleagues. They were thorough professionals. Their dedication towards work reflected in the clinical quiet of the office. I was getting serious too. This could last. I could see myself working there.

The gates to the office opened with my thumbprint. It was an event dramatic enough for me to commit. Or so I thought.

What did the British see when they looked at the plateau?

Around six kilometres from the present town lay a hill with several peaks. When viewed from the north, it appeared as a trident, but from the south, it revealed itself slowly, layer by layer, like a long-held secret. A miniature mountain range, this hill was locally called Juljul. Before 1857, a German man grew tea on its slopes.[5]

Juljul, with an elevation of 850 metres above sea level, would turn into a spectacle in monsoon and winter. When it rained, the clouds swallowed the peaks, leaving only the bust visible. The mists did the same in winter. Viewed from a distance, Juljul was an embodiment of sorrow, its summit wet and dripping.

'Mount Gloomy,' the British called it.[6]

They were considering the mountain as a potential site for a sanatorium. Whether the irony in constructing a sanatorium on a landmass called 'gloomy' was lost on them, I cannot say.

Juljul was the highest mountain near Hazaribagh. It may be a small mountain in itself, but its tallest peak is still a few hundred metres higher than the town. If Hazaribagh was perennially pleasant, a sanatorium on Juljul was bound to enjoy more favourable, *colder* temperatures.[7] Juljul was also the only landmass in Hazaribagh that was visible from as far as Kujju on the Ranchi Road. The mountain was emblematic, a potential symbol for the small, functional town which the British had planned and created.

To construct anything on top of Juljul was to stage a spectacle. They could not stage the spectacle.

Letters were exchanged between Hazaribagh and Calcutta. There were discussions about the availability of water, the estimate of residents, other logistical concerns. The plan almost came to fruition before it was abandoned suddenly and altogether. There was also a proposal for another sanatorium on Parasnath Hill. Both sanatoriums did well in the planning stage, both did not materialize. If water was a problem for Juljul, resistance from local tribesmen and Jain devotees was a bigger deterrent at Parasnath.[8]

Today, making anything on Juljul is impossible. The hill and its wilderness are protected by the forest laws. Paths masked with bushes and wild grass go up and along the mountain. What remain presently are the lantana shrubs, the trees and the caves deserted by tigers. Buddhist remains that the mountain occasionally reveals to the eye. Not a trace of Mr Leibart's tea plantation is visible today.

Villages have shifted closer to the foothills of Mount Gloomy, each house a sanatorium in itself.

On January 1, 2017, I was Mount Gloomy at New Delhi station.

The previous year, by December, I had lost count of the nights I spent without sleep. I often walked around obliviously and work, too, had turned mechanical. At the new office, a concerned senior suggested I do more physical activities.

'Take a long walk,' he advised, 'That way you will tire your body enough to fall asleep.' I walked across the flatness of Noida.

Upstairs in her cabin, another senior encouraged me to talk. We took personality tests, shared future plans. There was relief in sharing things with her.

My boss also stepped in and recommended a doctor.

I went to the clinic one evening and returned with a prescription later in the night.

Now that I think of it, I realize the futility of these exercises.

Despite love from all quarters, I was not getting better. My inability to recuperate frustrated me, prompting me to think I was betraying kindness that came my way. More than self-harm, I was terrified at the possibility of *romanticizing* my illness. I didn't know if returning home would offer a cure.

All I knew was that for some time at least I needed a sanctuary, perhaps that very sanatorium which was never built.

When the train reached Koderma the next morning, instead of a station from where I had boarded countless trains to Delhi in the past, I saw this time the plateau's flatland.

An hour ago, after the train had left Gaya, I had opened one of the coach's doors and sat down near the sink. It was still quite dark, but I could make out the silhouettes of hills rising before me. Cold, airy rapids made me shiver. I admired the *making* of the Chhotanagpur as the train travelled up the escarpment.

The sun had fallen behind its routine. The sky hadn't developed any reds yet. Then I realized it was winter, after all. *Silly, silly, depressed soul.* I witnessed the open country of Bihar transform within half an hour into dense forest and steep valleys, as dawn finally grew imminent over the locomotive. I saw the train curve through the three tunnels, each shorter than the one before it. When it rushed through

Gujhandi station without stopping, I saw the land open up again. The earth had changed its colour. The soil had turned into a corrupted shade of red, laterite.

When I stepped down at Koderma, I did so with the acute awareness of being in a different place. Alighting from the train, an event that had been so ordinary in the past, assumed a new significance. I was going to hold on to this, and if it was a mirage, I was going to wander into it nonetheless. I had little to lose.

I could not take the bus. I was carrying Delhi with me.

The city was packed in cartons, suitcases, backpacks. Thankfully, my mother, or Maate as I call her, had sent her Alto along with a driver whom I had met once or twice in Hazaribagh before. In the parking area, I saw the Citylink and BSF buses. I saw the men standing by jeep trekkers, hollering, '*Hajaaribaag*! *Hajaaribaag*! *Hajaaribaag*!'

With this familiar shout, they invited passengers descending the foot overbridge into their vehicles.

'*Hajaaribaag aaiye, Hajaaribaag aaiye, Hajaaribaag aaiye*! *Hajaaribaag, Hajaaribaag, Hajaaribaag*!'

When one man stopped for breath, another picked up.

I saw neon-lit betel shops going about their business. The affairs at the station were synced either to an auto-tuned piece of music or a Kumar Sanu melody. Homeless people had sheltered inside the unreserved waiting hall. Dogs were sleeping, squabbling and yawning on the sparse road outside.

The sixty-kilometre journey from Koderma to Hazaribagh is one from the Lower Chhotanapur to the Middle. I am fond of this road, which used to be narrower, beautifully shaded under the forest's canopy, and even more dramatic in its twists and turns a decade ago.

Like in many hill stations in India, the drive between Koderma and Hazaribagh is such where the traveller must leave the train at the nearest railhead and cover the remaining stretch by road.

Half an hour into the drive comes Urwan.

Till Urwan, nothing special happens. The plateau shows a patchwork of farmland, small ponds and minor rivers coursing through the hard flatland. The landscape is dotted with *dabba* or box-like buildings and houses. Families with less money leave the brickwork exposed. Families with more money paint the houses white. Families with lots of money paint the houses in bright shades of green, orange or purple.

At a distance, the chimneys of Koderma Thermal appear against the sky. The land is scrubby and uninspiring. So far.

After Urwan, the trees line up and the deception begins. Water flashes into view, as swiftly as it disappears. The low hills of Poraia Ridge rise ahead, rolling up, as if birthing straight from the uneven ground, and the road begins its dance. Running along the edges of the hill, it moves up the elevation, leaving the valley below to be swept away by the Barakar river. The highway curves, the highway turns, the highway acquires a body, limbs guided by each bend of the hill. The valley too culminates in the Barakar's huge reservoir. Buses, cars, and other vehicles shimmy along the road before they reach the bridge.

The bridge, or the channel of water below it, is the border.

In 1994, Koderma separated from Hazaribagh to become a district.

The famed mica of Hazaribagh, which in the nineteenth century was sent to the UK for its wallpaper industry, became the pride of Koderma. The 1953 Damodar Valley Corporation dam over the Barakar was inaugurated in Hazaribagh, but it now stands *officially* in Koderma. In this division, Koderma also got two waterfalls, Brindaha and Petro, along with the picturesque northern escarpment of the lower Chhotanagpur. While administrative boundaries are largely a function of governance and subject to change, I often find myself being petty and territorial about Hazaribagh. When I was a child, I would have many fights with my relatives over whether Patna or Muzaffarpur was better than Hazaribagh, or whether Bihar was better than Jharkhand, and I fought cruelly to keep my hometown and Jharkhand on top.

The winding road continues after the bridge too.

Hills that do not understand borders don't feel petty about their shoulders extending from one jurisdiction into another. *That* is unfortunately *my* thing. The forest thickens on the hill, while on the opposite side, the view of Barakar becomes complete. The sun appears over the reservoir. The water holds a vain mirror up to it.

This sight belongs to Hazaribagh, even if Koderma got the concrete wall of the dam.

The road cleaves a path through the range, staging the final reveal of the view ahead, before tumbling down into the flatland beyond. This is Barhi. Our road, the NH 33, meets the old Grand Trunk Road of the cunning tigers here. The spell is over.

Cinderella has returned to her plain clothes.

Moderation is the key word.

In the plateau here, moderation works as an anti-thesis to the sublime. No view, no extensive landscape, no thrilling drive can sustain for long.

The highland, to use its admirer Thompson's word, is 'broken'. It reveals beauty in pockets; much of Jharkhand is like this. These breaks, interruptions, scatter the charm across the whole plateau: no part is left without its own small treasure. There is little excess, nothing spills over, and I struggle to reconcile with this fact.

As a student of literature, I am conditioned to think that art exists *in excess*, that beauty which escapes from its closet is most delightful, so I get insecure when the plateau turns my presumption on its head. The mockery brings disappointment, and later, reconciliation. Disappointment, because when I photograph the hills, waterfalls and valleys, I inadvertently look for the superlative: *the tallest, the highest, the deepest*. What the plateau returns to me is usually a superlative for my approach: *the shallowest*.

When both of us have accepted our adjectives, we return to being friends again.

I was on the road, eyes open, moving my head left and right to absorb the gravity of my decision to return home.

'When will you be back?' A friend had asked in Delhi.

'I hope I don't have to be back, at least not like this,' I confessed.

It was a difficult parting, cloaked under farewell parties and gifts.

The Alto had crossed Barhi and now we were about to leave Padma behind as well.

Padma was the last capital of Ramgarh Raj. The palace along with its Hawa Mahal for queens is presently in ruins. The sun above was gradually maturing in the sky. In its light, I tried to spot the Hawa Mahal's yellow dome behind newer constructions.

These recent buildings belong to the Jharkhand Armed Police Training Academy, but still, from the highway, if only for a few seconds, the dome was visible. When I spotted it, its colour mud-like, I remembered a joke that's thrown around in Hazaribagh. Noting the extent of its decay, some people have now started suggesting that Padma Palace should be renamed *Sadma* Palace.

'*Wahaan jaane se sadma lagta hai*, it's painful,' they say.

This is true. It's traumatic for the people who go to see it. I'm sure it's traumatic also for the building to be seen in such misery.

If the stretch from Barhi to Padma was ordinary, I was preparing myself for another magical stretch. Not once have I crossed the forest of Hazaribagh National Park without being awestruck by the sal trees.

Sal trees are a symbol of Jharkhand. They grow tall and they shoot straight. In the warmer regions, sal trees turn the landscape into a lush, sensory feast. The trees turn roads into neat passes, they give scale to the view. When the season changes, their leaves acquire different colours and the forest scintillates.

The forest of the national park is also the slyest escarpment of the plateau. Since the trees obstruct the view on either side of the road, one does not really notice the slowly rising ground. A slight change in temperature occurs here. Hazaribagh loyalists call this phenomenon *gulabi thand*, or the pink chill.

I waited in the car, windows rolled down in the January winter, for the fresh chill to hit me. When it did, I felt it on my elbow. I couldn't help but smile.

This was it.

The hill station is ageing. This becomes apparent when I read the signboard welcoming the incoming traffic into town.

It does not refer to Hazaribagh as 'the land of a thousand gardens' or '*hazaar baaghon ka shehar*,' the meaning which the word carries *by default*. Instead, it defines the town in a dull, administrative register.

Uttari Chhotanagpur Pramandal ke mukhyalaya
Hazaribagh shehar me aapka swagat hai.

Welcome to Hazaribagh, the headquarters of the North
Chhotanagpur Division.

Hazaribagh is not an organic name of the town, which is only about 250 years old. The name was a *conscious*, creative intervention. It was coined by purposefully joining two words together. It is poetic, again, *by default*.

I do not understand what I am supposed to do with the *Uttari Chhotanagpur Pramandal* when I can really have a thousand gardens. I also do not understand what people from other places who come to Hazaribagh are supposed to do with the *Uttari Chhotanagpur Pramandal*. Not once have

I been identified elsewhere by my *Uttari Chhotanagpur Pramandal*-iya descent.

Meanwhile in Jharkhand, other poetic places have emerged. On the road to Netarhat, the signboard states, '*Jharkhand ka gaurav Netarhat me aapka swagat hai*'. The pride of Jharkhand Netarhat welcomes you. In south Jharkhand, I see '*Saranda ki vaadiyon me aapka swagat hai*'. The valleys of Saranda welcome you.

I admire Netarhat and Saranda. They are lush, misty and stunning places. I am fond of them too. But the slow detachment of poetic and pastoral values from Hazaribagh's identity and imagination troubles me.

When I consider the signage as *text*, I see an active erasure of history, an erasure of poetry too. The history of administration in Hazaribagh started *because* of the plateau and its landscape, not in spite of it. Its recent identification as merely a 'headquarters' town marks a fundamental shift in its perception. It tells me that Hazaribagh could soon be another Tier-3 city with its made-up parks, ersatz ponds, token forest, shorn increasingly of its inherent beauty.

In the last stretch of my journey back home, when it was no longer dawn, the sun no longer weak, I wondered romantically if there was a connection between my life and that of Hazaribagh as a retreat town. I thought perhaps when I die, the hill station too will go with me. But when the Alto passed by the Deputy Commissioner's residence, I remembered I was not the first one to have such thoughts.

Samuel Solomon, a former DC of Hazaribagh, was also a poet.

In 1946, he wrote a long poem titled 'Garden at

Hazaribagh', which he published as a small, pocket-size book of verse.

In the poem, thinking clearly about his future, his post-independence life, he ponders a question which haunts him repeatedly.

'Will this loveliness stay after we are gone?' Solomon wants to know.

The poem is a guided tour of his garden. He shows us the 'jacaranda boughs', the lilies, the cannas. Throughout the poem, he demonstrates how pleasure obtained by accessing, crafting and participating with the land can root a person to it. Therefore, the resulting nostalgia, and in the end, an optimism for the future.

'This loveliness shall stay after we are gone,' Solomon finishes his poem, departing but hopeful.

The reason I invoke Solomon here is to show that administration and beauty have worked together sympathetically for over two centuries in Hazaribagh.

Solomon, besides being a poet, was an administrator himself.

I have gradually begun to echo Solomon's sentiments.

To be in Hazaribagh today is to see the hill station treading between extinction and survival. Yet, newer, creative articulations keep bringing the plateau back. And this is important: to recognize Hazaribagh first and foremost as a plateau, and not a hill. The growing interest in photography and local tourism has pushed people outwards into the land, and now I find many photos of forests and streams dotting my Facebook feed.

On the other hand, a seductive, dangerous kind of nostalgia also attaches itself easily to Hazaribagh. Nostalgia may be a form of appreciation, but often it is also a convenient rhetoric, a condescending, detached gaze directed at the present.

If Hazaribagh did not disappear after Solomon, it will not disappear after me either. Perhaps the town *will* become a city, perhaps it *will* become the headquarters of a larger *pramandal* or something equally important.

When I returned to Hazaribagh, I did not particularly return to write this book, at least not in this form. I had returned simply to heal myself.

'Why do you want to be an adman, or even a professor for that matter?' My friend Geetika had once asked me in Delhi.

It was a pensive evening. One where I sat quietly and listened.

'In this city, you will be one among thousands. Are *you* one among the thousands? You already know what you have to do, so go ahead and do it.

'Here, you are replaceable. If not someone, then you. If not you, then someone else. There are so many copywriters, so many professors. Don't you see the crowd that piles up for every interview at every college? Are you part of the *crowd*?'

What do you do when your friend's belief in you surpasses your own?

'You, Mihir, are a writer. The way you feel about Hazaribagh, I don't think anyone else does. So travel, make memories, meet people. Write.

'You can always return to the routine later.'

The two-and-a-half years I spent in Hazaribagh after returning from Delhi were not routine. They were spent in travelling, making memories, meeting people, and trying to understand what precisely made the plateau beautiful. When the experiences piled up, the necessity for this book became apparent.

This book, therefore, is about me *and* the Hazaribagh Plateau. It is also about me *in* the Hazaribagh Plateau. It is not about the town, but the land. And though it does delve into history, it is not a history book. Hazaribagh's local history, besides documented events, is more a lore, passed down through generations, invoked in conversations, open to myth-making. In January 2017, I was no longer looking to 'do something' for Hazaribagh. The plateau had only just opened up.

It was doing things to me.

Hill

I have come to appreciate a new revelation.

It is concerned with the naming of things.

Take a stream and chart its route till it becomes a river.

As water assumes a body, villages and towns birth close to it. The water travels not only through its course over the land, but also through generations of people who watch it, who are raised by it, and who *personalize* it. They take the river to their homes in pots and buckets, through irrigation pumps slaking the fields, in water that sticks to their feet as they enter through the doors.

They include the river in their stories, they make songs about it, they give the river a *culture*.

Some drown when the river floods and this makes for a tragic story. Some survive through luck or bravery, and we get to read about it in the newspapers the next day.

Through all the settlements that this water moves, it is given names, and occasionally, epithets. The Damodar becomes in Jharkhand its 'lifeline', though for a long time it was Bengal's 'sorrow'.

Sometimes the names change with places, like the Konar river of Hazaribagh becomes Lara Nadi near Lara village, or the rustic Muhane in Jharkhand becomes a more sophisticated Mohana in Bihar.

Like Lara Nadi, the names often refer to the nearest inhabited locations, and like the Bokaro and the Barakar, the rivers end up giving names to their nearest towns.

Since naming is intricately connected to identity, identity to culture, and culture to *chronology*, a name in human societies ceases to be an innocent assembly of letters. It becomes an artefact of time and space.

In the north-eastern part of Hazaribagh town rises a high mass of rocks, boulders, soil, bushes and trees. A pink laterite road circumambulates it and tall sal trees stand as guards on either side. This is not the Juljul, but a different hill.

As soon as I leave the town's tarmac road and enter the woods, the temperature takes a dip. The noise of traffic quietens down, at first to a soft hum, then recedes completely from my mind. A new soundscape takes over, comprising bird calls, the crunch of gravel beneath my shoes, and the rustling of leaves when a breeze starts from one part of the forest and moves to the other.

This landmass, whose top is accessed by 570 or so steps and which leaves a blanket of forest trailing in the east, has been called by many names.

In 1813, when Captain Robert Smith, an engineer with the East India Company, came to Hazaribagh, he climbed up the hill, cleared a nice spot for himself, and drew a sketch of what he saw: a wide forest extending into the country which then disappeared into a cluster of hills near Silwar village. This was the time when tigers were alive in the forest of Hazaribagh.

When Smith finished the sketch, which wasn't elaborate or detailed, he captioned it, 'Part of Tiger Hill and Seilwar Hill dist. near Hazareebaugh'.

And so, Tiger Hill came into existence.

That the British were a homesick people in India is a fact well-known.

Annoyed by the climate of Calcutta, they looked for places that could give them some semblance of home. Where semblance was scarce, they looked for shadows.

Smith's Tiger Hill, when viewed in profile, offered a resemblance to the Rock of Gibraltar.

Though there was no Mediterranean seafront to Tiger Hill in Hazaribagh, its altitude—600 metres above sea level and 200 metres more than the Rock—seemed to have made up for the water's absence. The British took to it readily, and it wasn't long that Smith's Tiger Hill acquired the nickname Gibraltar.

Detached from its colonial nomenclature, the natives who were mostly forest-dwelling Santhals, called the hill Kunhuri, meaning an arrowhead. By the time the British left, the hill already had its fourth name, which it still carries: Canary.

Thousands of miles away from the famous Canary Islands, and with no connection to the bird either, the name Canary is an anglicised version of—and yet separate from—the vernacular Kanhari.

So when I talk about the hill in Hindi, it is always

Kanhari, and when I talk about the hill in English, it is always Canary. I cannot think of Kanhari Hill in English, and I cannot think of Canary Pahad in Hindi.

In Indian classrooms, we are programmed to view hills as physical geography, but if this brief history of Canary's multiple names points to anything, it is to the fact that hills like this are also important cultural entities.

Canary, like Juljul, is also a trickster, a shape-shifter of a hill.

When viewed from the west, it takes the form of a sharp triangle out of a high school student's geometry notebook. The fall from the top is sharp, if not sheer.

When viewed from the east, the triangle dwarfs in altitude. It becomes stepped and broad at the base, looking like the rear end of a Maruti Swift.

From the south, it is a trapezium with four corners, two rooted in the land and the other two propped up against the sky.

From the north, it is the profile of a woman standing in a forest, her sari trailing behind in a green, gentle descent. Quite like the heroines we see in Yash Raj Films and Dharma Productions movies.

Canary, like Juljul, is also a *view in motion*, and no two views are the same.

In the monsoon, a low mist collects at its base, lending the hill a spell of levitation. In winters, a high mist shrouds the summit, and Canary looks as if it rose so high up in the sky that it was simply swallowed by the space.

To us, who know some history of the hill, and to those who have spent time with it, the story of Canary is that of enduring fondness and perpetual degeneration.

Part of its pessimism is born out of an irrational but *tender* romance for the past, a past that must compulsively remain glorious. All generations of people maintain that Canary was the most beautiful in their time; all generations maintain that Canary was the most tragic in their time.

I spend my years, oblivious, and with time, remember the past as golden too.

Like many British administrators before him, Sir John Wardle Houlton was an admirer of Hazaribagh.

For this former Deputy Commissioner, Hazaribagh was 'a quiet back-water' residing in its lovely solitude, located miles away from the nearest railway station. This detachment from modern civilization rendered a timeless quality to Hazaribagh.

Though sometimes I grudgingly feel that the higher escarpment of Ranchi Plateau and the scenery it offers is more impressive, Houlton felt the opposite. Not only did he consider Hazaribagh's landscape more attractive than Ranchi's, he envisioned a future for the town as a 'health-resort for the people of the plains of Bengal and Bihar.'

When I google Hazaribagh, often out of curiosity to see how the town is being described for the outside world, the results declare the place a 'health-resort'.

This is Houlton's phrase, which he had used in his 1949 book, *Bihar: The Heart of India*. Houlton had used the phrase to articulate only a possibility for the town, but for better or worse, it is now etched permanently in the perception of the place.

In recent years, I have met many curious folks who have come to Hazaribagh looking for a lavish resort, located perhaps by the lake or in the foothills of Canary, and after not finding any, returning disappointed. They missed the whole point. The town *is* the resort.

Houlton was drawn to the forest of Canary too. During his tenure as the DC, he saw in the jungle, besides leopards and jungle fowl, a *city forest* way before the concept gained its modern currency. He planned a park at the foot of the hill and he carved out a small pond on its southern face. When it brimmed with water, he put fish into it.

In the larger scheme of things, Houlton's hope was to turn the forest into a 'national park in miniature'.

There are many reasons for a forest to be conserved or protected.

Earlier, it was done for timber or hunting, later to preserve wildlife. Today, the principal utility of a forest, or anything green for that matter, gravitates towards ensuring that we inhale better air.

Houlton's need for conserving his miniature national park stemmed from hunting, but he went a step further and linked it to knowledge. He had hoped that in the future, people would come not merely to enjoy the unspoilt views of his game reserve but also to learn a thing or two about 'that great natural asset, the forests of India.'

Canary's golden past also refers to the time of SP Shahi, a legendary forest officer of undivided Bihar. Both Houlton and Shahi deserve credit for making Canary accessible to the people.

If Houlton was focussed on the forest, roughly a decade

later, Shahi looked straight up at the hill. In the 1950s, as Bihar's Conservator of Forest, he commissioned a number of constructions on Canary. He built a forest rest house on the hill's east face, and the iconic shelter on the west. However, to build a shelter at the top meant also constructing a stairway up the hill.

Huge boulders were removed and patches of vegetation cleared to make way for a bare, narrow strip to coil up the hill. Later, brickwork commenced along this strip to create stairs. For climbers to rest, concrete benches were placed along the route.

It must have been a grind for Shahi's men, and to some people at the time, it must also have amounted to the destruction of a landmass that had, for so long, stayed untouched.

Houlton was enterprising, but even he had spared the hill.

In fact, there's a chapter in writer Malay Kumar Roy's Hazaribagh memoir, *An Elsewhere Place*, which tells us about a man who grew so disheartened at the human encroachment of Canary through roads and buildings, through dynamite explosions, that he vowed never to return. He was not seen again, ever.

The white shelter at the top of Canary, accessed by 570 or so steps, commanded Hazaribagh's sky.

It consolidated the shape of the hill into a more apparent pyramid. It turned what was initially a curved top into a neat peak.

Shahi did not stop at the shelter.

A gentle shoulder on the east was levelled into an incline,

and a forest rest house was raised overlooking Houlton's game reserve. Lastly, the petite rest house was given its own observation tower, a remarkable yet simple structure which has stood on a titanic boulder ever since its construction.

When I go there to watch the sunrise, I observe Houlton's forest. I also observe Captain Smith's cluster of hills at Silwar. I observe the town half-asleep and half-awake. I see athletes on their morning run. I see middle-aged men and women doing Yoga or Pranayaam.

With the shelter on the west, a rest house on the east, and a road that circled Canary in the fashion of a holy parikrama, I cannot help but wonder if Shahi realized the weight of what he was doing.

Besides initiating a landscape development project, Shahi was turning Canary into a future pilgrimage.

However, his white shelter, which loomed over the town like an omnipresent temple, was meant not for divinity but people. Canary was made sacred, it was made *democratic*, and it was done for the service of the visitors.

By opening Canary up to Hazaribagh, Shahi had turned a landmass into a landmark, and how!

At the foothills of Canary is the DAV School where I studied.

During the six years I spent there, the hill was an indelible presence in my student life along with my books, my teachers and my friends. All the classrooms that were allotted to my section offered views of the hill. Whether in regular classes or during exams, Canary was the cause of, and a shelter from, my many distractions. It lured me into taking discreet breaks from whatever teaching was going on, and at times of confusion during tests, its sight aided contemplation.

In the initial years, the bus brought me to school, to the hill, and it also took me home. Later, it was my bicycle.

The main route to the school is through the Canary Hill Road.

It starts from SP Kothi, the residence of the district's Superintendent of Police, and ends at the hill. The journey *up* to the school is actually a journey *down* to the hill.

Canary Hill Road was once a stretch where prosperous families built their holiday homes in Hazaribagh. These were second homes for people who lived elsewhere, mostly in the plains of Bihar and Bengal.

Cycling through this road, I saw several bungalows and villas.

There was the Kona Kothi, the corner bungalow, called so because it was located in a secluded corner by the road. There was Canary Villa, which is now in ruins and its public view screened off by a row of shops. There was the Sanctoria, a single-storey, modern and sleek construction, which belonged to one Ramaiyajee Verma. Further ahead, there was the pink Balaka, the daintiest bungalow of all, which belonged to a Dr. Lahiri who, as the lore went, 'lived in England.'

There is a culture in India of aspiring for places of high altitude, notably among the country's middle-classes. I have not been able to put my finger on the exact reasons for this, but I do think about it often.

I understand the British fixation with the hills in India, but this feeling of being at home in high places among *us* seems to me an example of colonial conditioning, of one culture spilling onto another.

The bungalows on Canary Hill Road have a quality of aspiration to them, a desire to show off wealth in a tangible, theatrical manner. There is also detachment from the ordinary, crowded town.

In its prime, the road down to the hill must have looked like a procession of prosperous homes. I would rather not judge this theatre, as I too am a product of the same cultural milieu. When my penniless days are over, hopefully, and I too get the chance to make a house by a hill, I probably will.

What I am trying to say is that a hill may be a cultural entity, but that culture is grounded in *class*. There is a difference between those who come to see the hill for a few hours and those who come to, and can afford to, live by it.

This procession along the Canary Hill Road ends at a regal mansion.

This mansion confounded me. In fact, it confounded all my friends. It was a building that was neither impressive nor inviting.

Possibly the earliest home to be built on this road, its setting was choreographed in a way that could only evoke awe. The structure was almost always hidden behind a shield of trees, so it seemed like the house had its own forest.

We did not see one soul enter through the gates, we did not see anyone emerge out of them either. Yet the bungalow was not decrepit. It never seemed to fall into disrepair.

I personally thought the building was haunted. If not

ghosts, then maybe an old witch lived there. How else could the manor be so properly kept, when there were no signs of life around it?

We concocted several stories, my friends and I, and though we maintained our distance from the house, it exerted a strange pull on us. We knew there was no match for it in Hazaribagh. The other houses may have been huge, they may have been gigantic or sporting all sorts of attractive embellishments. But they weren't half as regal as this one.

When I was a child, my geography was limited.

Hazaribagh was my kingdom and this manor was the king's palace. It was home to a Justice SC Mallick of Calcutta. A neat marble plaque embedded on the gatepost told us this much. Above the Justice's name was inscribed the name of the building.

Gibraltar.

The first time I entered the premises of Gibraltar, it was dark.

I had not been personally invited to the house, but the person I was driving there was.

After the wrought iron gates opened in the night, my Alto, suddenly aware of its headlights unsettling the darkness of the place, moved nervously up the gravel driveway. Under the beaming lights, it seemed as if a chimera from the horizon had slowly zoomed up to the sky. The headlights fell first over the base of the building, illuminating the faded red foundation over which the manor stood, and as the path levelled up, Gibraltar filled out in its totality and glared curiously at the vehicle.

In the night, the darkness of the estate was not an impediment. It was its essence. It *privatized* the house and protected it. The mansion and the land were in on the performance together: to imagine one without the other would be to foil the Gibraltar's imagination.

The person I was driving was Bulu Imam, then seventy-six years old, my very own *age-inappropriate* friend.

His work in the field of heritage conservation in Jharkhand had earned him the Gandhi International Peace Prize in 2011, and subsequently in 2019, the Padma Shri. I call him Bulu Uncle. He is a man of many stories and my preferred authority on Hazaribagh's history. I actually learned about SP Shahi and the construction of the watchtower on top of the hill from Uncle during one of our evening talks. We have known each other for the past ten years, and I have joined him often in lamenting the degradation of Hazaribagh.

With him the past is glorious, the present morose, the future hopeless.

I was an accidental visitor to Gibraltar.

Earlier that evening, I had come to see Uncle at his house in Dipugarha, after returning from the beautiful hill village of Jorakath, south of Hazaribagh. The Imams had organized a Christmas fete in the grounds, but I had arrived late and all the good stuff on the menu was gone.

Left to my consolatory tea, I decided to hover close to Uncle as he met with the guests. It was then that he mentioned Gibraltar. He was expected there. A man called

Debabrata and a woman called Ayesha had come from Kolkata. They were cousins. Gibraltar was their home. Uncle was to spend some time with them, after which he had other engagements.

Was there a car around? Plenty.

Was there a driver around?

I saw Justin, his eldest son, already occupied with the fete. I saw him dashing around the grounds, trying to make sure that things were going well.

'I could drive you,' I offered.

Before entering the mansion, Bulu Uncle wanted to show me something. We walked around the building, west, south and then east, and came to the backyard.

As I saw for the first time the eastern facade of Gibraltar, I gaped at the tall white columns which I had not seen before.

'Very Doric,' I observed quietly, turning back every now and then to look.

In the dark, I also grew increasingly aware of this trespassing, but since Uncle was around, I was not worried. We climbed up and down the boulders and came to the edge of the elevation, upon which the manor stood.

Below us, there were uprooted trees, trunks piled up on one side, and an unnaturally wide clearing. It was a site of sadness.

'This is where they are building the new road from,' Uncle informed me.

There was only one source of light with us, his torch. Whatever I could see, I saw. What I could not, I deduced.

'You won't believe what one Babu told them when they

asked him to build the road from behind the forest,' Uncle resumed.

'He said, "But we are clearing all your *jhaadi*-jungle for free! What problem could you have with that?"'

We laughed in the dark.

Uncle and I belong to the coterie that trusts *jhaadi*-jungle more than people.

'I am telling you, Mihir,' his voice was strained, 'you cannot talk sense to an ass. You cannot teach Aristotle to a donkey. The donkey will live. You, my young friend, will not.'

In India people are, simultaneously, both Aristotle and the ass.

When we returned from our detour, we found the housekeeper holding out a torch and looking in our direction. As we drew closer, he recognized Uncle and took us inside.

He opened another wrought iron gate, much smaller this time, and we walked through a doorway. Inside, I saw the high ceiling, the grey cement floor, the white walls. I saw overground wiring, a black wooden stairway, minimal lighting. I saw shuttered windows, the cubicle of a pantry, the framed artworks.

I saw it all and I knew that I had travelled through time, into something far greater than myself.

In the huge sitting room upstairs, Uncle spoke with Ayesha and Debabrata, the house's human residents. I scanned the air for ghosts and poltergeists. When I found no paranormal presence, I returned my attention to where we were seated.

Beside me was a brilliant fireplace that warded off the cold. This was my third active fireplace sighting in Hazaribagh. Ayesha handled it expertly, turning the wood at just the right moment to keep the fire going.

'I can never keep it going,' I remarked, holding my glass of coke.

Uncle was enjoying his whiskey.

I told Ayesha about a night I once spent with a friend at the Hazaribagh National Park.

We had enough wood to keep the fire running through the night, but neither of us knew *how* to actually do it. It had been an embarrassing realization for us, and after the fire died, we had to abandon our engrossing chat and go to bed, much against our wishes.

'We have been coming here since we were kids,' Ayesha said.

'In the winter, we had to learn to keep the fire going. That is how I learned, that's how all of us learned.'

The general conversation in the room was beyond my participation.

Uncle spoke with the cousins about mutual friends and the old days. Their old days always sounded irritatingly better than mine. My own old days, comprising twenty-seven winters at that time, were unremarkable.

Left to my own devices, observing the room and chatting occasionally with Ayesha, I also began to notice how very ordinary Gibraltar was. That instead of a haunted shell, it was a giant home where people *actually* lived. It was as banal in its functioning as my home. It was a space where people talked, where they laughed, where they exchanged disappointments. It was where people offered whiskey to those who drank whiskey, and coke to those who did not. I noticed that at Gibraltar, fire too was sustained.

I had learned from *Aahat*, and other nineties' horror TV shows, that ghosts were scared of fire. So eyeing the lasting embers, I was convinced that the only presence in the house was ours. Not scared anymore, I sat cosy beside the fire as Uncle, Ayesha and Debabrata continued their conversation.

On that fateful night, I saw the manor transform into what Justice Mallick, Ayesha's grandfather, in 1911, must have thought it would be: a home.

Besides bringing Gibraltar out from its idyllic seclusion to immediate exposure, what else did the new road do?

For the longest time, the new bypass road had stopped right before the forest.

From the north, it bifurcated from the existing highway at Sindoor, and from the south, it broke off from the Konar Bridge at Masipirhi, found Gibraltar on the way, and stopped. Like an abrupt ceasefire, both these arms of the new road halted at the forest.

I would hear tales flying about the delay in their union: the forest department wasn't giving clearance, there was a court case, the perennial '*thekedaar bhaag gaya*' stories and so on. I assumed that the courts, being courts, would sit on the matter for maybe another decade or so.

Sometimes, returning from my walks, I spoke with people who lived *with* the hill. I do not remember anyone being particularly enthusiastic about the proposed alignment of the road. Even the most pro-'development' lot felt uneasy at the sight of development happening so close to their homes.

They knew that the reasons for which they had come to live with the hill would no longer be there, once the road came through. Already the air was heavy with dust, the existing road turning ugly with the movement of giant trucks and dumpers. When it rained, brown mud heaped by the road would turn into sludge and take over the tarmac, as if the earth had languidly puked it up.

Canary's immediate neighbours couldn't enjoy the same quiet of the forest anymore, nor could they get the hill's clean air. Sometimes, driven by frustration, I posted inconsequential rants about this on Facebook. Sometimes, while conducting nature walks with my friend, the entomologist Mrityunjay Sharma, we explained to participants that anywhere between 1,500 to 3,000 trees were destined for death in this exercise.

I have not yet met one person who was enthusiastic about the construction of the road at the cost of dead trees. Many, like me, know that except for Canary's forest, there exists no sizable wilderness in the town. The closest forests are located along the plateau's escarpment, all fifteen to twenty-five kilometres away.

The new road, therefore, will always beg the question upon its genesis: which illuminated mind, already living under the threat of climate change, came up with the idea to build the road through the woods?

When the trees were marked for felling, they were assigned numbers.

Small rectangular patches were carved out on trunks by removing the bark, so that the yellow layer underneath was visible to the eyes.

Till the time the ceasefire was in place, I would venture unnoticed into this arboreal graveyard. It was like visiting a friend or a relative on life-support. I knew their death was inevitable, yet I went to see the trees, as if I were paying my last respects.

I had not bothered to enter this part of the forest before, sticking mostly to the routine of the circular road and the stairs that went up the hill. However, after I steered away from the road one morning and decided to go into the forest, an element of guilt began to work inside me.

'You are just being cute,' it said. 'A performative millennial, that's all.'

I may have indeed been a performative millennial in the forest.

Everyone starts off by being a little performative, but my performance was earnest.

After walking north through the trees and bushes for some time, I arrived at a clearing. When I looked back to see the route I had taken, I was greeted with a view of Canary I had never seen before.

In one slanting line, I saw Shahi's shelter descend to the radio tower, which then went down to the part of the hill that supported the Forest Rest House. The rest house wasn't visible, but the outline of the hill was so clear, it seemed as if I were looking at Canary for the very first time. Not very far from that clearing, slightly away from its centre, was a tree that I liked a lot.

It was a sal tree and its number was 1362.

I went to see 1362 often.

I would rise early and make sure to be inside the forest before the hill swarmed with joggers and morning walkers.

Before dawn broke, I would be in, making my way to the clearing. Paths in the forest hardly run parallel, I came to learn soon, after getting lost a couple of times. Once I saw a dead hare, its pelt decaying and stuck to the ground. Then, on the same day, I saw another hare, alive and leaping across the trail. *Sighting wildlife at Canary now?* I was amused.

To say that I was growing fond of the forest would be an example of language trivialising an emotion. I remember the day when Sumana Roy's book *How I Became a Tree* arrived at home. I had taken it to Canary, to 1362, and leaning against the trunk, I read a chapter aloud. There was love blossoming in the Arden, between me and the doomed tree. It was tragic from the beginning. The forest would soon be a stretch of tar.

I had begun to love the tree at the wrong time. I, a fucking performative millennial.

I have come to appreciate a new revelation.

It is concerned with consolation in things.

There are so many things that have changed at Canary, but there are also things that have not.

Things that haven't changed at Canary:

The sharp morning light reflecting off the shiny gravel on the laterite road, the sharp morning light allowed passage by the trees to touch the laterite road, the sharp morning light absorbed by the skin on our bodies as we walk on the laterite road.

Things that haven't changed at Canary:

Houlton's pond. There are so many fish in it today, they take a boat through the tiny lake, catching them in nets.

Things that haven't changed at Canary:

Teenagers desperate for a quick drag on a cigarette, students climbing up and down the hill after an exam gets over, carrying on a tradition started by our seniors. Lovers scribbling their names on the rocks.

Things that haven't changed at Canary:

Smith's view of the hills at Silwar, which is shared by so many people today, the curiosity surrounding the forest rest house: *how does one get to stay here?*

Things that haven't changed at Canary:

The yellowing teak leaves in October, the red sal leaves in March, a few odd casuarinas that have survived both the British and the Indians.

Things that haven't changed at Canary:

The birdcalls, the conversations, the hill's *sociality*, its quality of facilitating meetings, and its resistance to entertain the superfluous demands of a 'tourist spot'.

The canteen at Canary never functioned and it probably never will. Dewy-eyed administrators return dejected when the hill itself vetoes further beautification, or as we say in these parts, *sundarikaran*. Bring your own food. Bring your own water.

The hill, sometimes, is only a hill. It is this hill which we climb. It is this hill on which our sweat falls.

I started from home at five-thirty. It was summer, so it wouldn't be properly dark before seven. I usually took about half an hour, maybe forty-five minutes, to climb all the stairs. In the bag, I kept my camera. In one of my hands, I held the tripod.

The first time my friend Rizwan Ashraf and I had photographed the night-time view of town from the top, it was 2013. We used to do all kinds of silly stuff with the camera and the accessories back then. I would model for him often, by the trunk of a tree, or at my home.

Now Rizwan was married and in Bangalore, and five years later, I was keen to see the view again.

Leaving the Alto by the defunct canteen, I started climbing up.

After a hundred steps, the first wave of fatigue set in. It was all too familiar. I had climbed the hill so many times, I knew the points of slack.

By the halfway mark, the town began to assemble beneath the hill. The high winds woke up. No electric lights yet. The sky was still bright, the sun still lingering. On the next flight of stairs, I passed a group of teenagers returning from the shelter. Very few people from the town climb Canary to see Hazaribagh in the dark. Half an hour before the lights are turned on, the hill is usually deserted. Seeing the boys therefore was a surprise. I thought I would be alone on the top, but I couldn't be sure anymore. There might be more people up there.

When I reached the first table shelter, I found to my disappointment more boys. They spoke loudly and excitedly with each other. They laughed with full hearts and did little to preserve the quiet of the hill. Aggravated, I moved up to the second temple shelter. This was empty. I released the tripod to its full frame, fixed my Nikon upon it, and started my first round of photography.

The sun had lost its glare and was now a crimson ball suspended in the sky. The wind was welcome at first, but it soon turned cruel. Sharp gusts tested the trees and the clash howled all around. Inside the shelter, I held the tripod firmly, stopping it from toppling over. Quickly, it also grew chilly. The town below was screened by a layer of haze, which annoyed me. It emanated from the construction of the new road at Sindoor. The visibility on that side of the town was poor.

My camera and tripod must have attracted the boys below, because soon they had all joined me in the shelter. 'So much for the alone time...' I muttered under my breath. There was nothing I could do. I may dislike a crowd, but I am not a tyrant. Besides, I can barely scare a fly with my face, let alone a bunch of teenagers.

The boys were not exactly from Hazaribagh town.

They were from Barkattha, an administrative block of the district and a small town located about fifty kilometres from Canary.

They were all around sixteen years old. They had just passed their tenth board exams and had come to what, for them, was a city.

'It's our first day in Hazaribagh! We were getting bored, so someone told us to climb the hill,' they informed me gleefully.

I instantly took a liking to that unnamed someone. Climbing Canary is one of the better ways to see Hazaribagh.

'We are here to do coaching,' they said.

I was learning too.

As we talked amongst each other, the twelve of us up on the hill, the sun finally dipped. Looking at the sky, they felt it was time to go.

'We should be leaving,' they said.

Whenever I remember this evening, the boys speak to me in a chorus.

I may have initially been irked by their presence, but since it was their first day in town, I suggested that they stay back a little longer to see Hazaribagh in the night. 'Now that you have spent an hour here, you better stay for another half.'

Heeding my advice, five boys from the group stayed back while the remaining six took off.

As expected, fifteen minutes later, the town's light show started.

It wasn't completely dark yet. We could still make out the buildings and the colours of paint. I started with my camera. They resumed their chattering.

'Did you see that fellow at Columba's today? He was laughing like an idiot, ha ha ha ha.'

'You have a girlfriend, don't you? No *you* have a girlfriend! No *you* have a girlfriend, ha ha ha ha ha'.

'Hey, did he call home? Do you know what his father told him? If he did any more *alar-balar* in Hazaribagh, *toh* he would take him straight back to Barkattha, ha ha ha ha ha.'

Quietly, I stood in a corner with my camera and tried not to show that I was laughing too. When the night took over, the town below turned into a conference of stars. The forest below remained blissfully dark. We saw the darkness set in, we saw the lights come up. When I had my photos, I showed them to the boys.

'Oooo, so nice, fantastic!' they said, again in a chorus.

When we came back down to where I had parked the Alto, I offered to drop them to their lodge at Korrah. They jumped in without hesitation. It was almost eight in the night, there was no way they were going to get an auto from Canary. On the way, they started quizzing me.

'What do you do?'

I told them I was a photographer. 'I take photos of hills and forests.'

I don't think they were impressed. I wasn't either. When we arrived at Korrah, they asked me to drop them at the crossroads.

'We can go from here, thank you very much.'

I said it was okay.

'No, you don't understand. This was our first day in Hazaribagh. So far, we had only met rude people.'

It was clear they were grateful for the ride back home.

'We didn't think Hazaribagh had people like you.'

I was getting embarrassed sitting in the driver's seat.

'There are people like me everywhere,' I said. 'If it was someone else on the hill, they would have done the same.'

'No,' one of the boys interjected, 'they wouldn't. That's why we are thankful.'

I couldn't bear the sincerity in their words anymore.

'*Achcha*, now go to your lodge, all of you. I will see you around.'

When I reached home, I had already received friend requests from them on Facebook.

One of the boys was called Ajit. He wrote me a message in English, confessing that he was too homesick in Hazaribagh and that he wanted to go back to Barkattha. 'It is very new for me.'

I understood homesickness all too well to reply with a platitude.

I told him about my childhood, how before joining DAV, I too had lived in a boarding school.

'I was four when I was sent to the hostel. You are sixteen,' I typed.

My reply seemed to calm him.

'How did you manage?' he asked.

'You learn,' I said. 'You learn to make your bed, you learn to wash your clothes, you learn to cook your food.'

He said he realized in Hazaribagh that washing clothes was too tiring an activity.

'Well,' I said, 'Didn't you only tell me on the hill that you were here for coaching? I don't think you can do that in Barkattha.'

I told him that his homesickness would pass and he would come to enjoy it here. This was hypocritical, of course, because what I said to him was completely opposite to what I had done myself.

The seven years I lived in Delhi had turned me into a 'Dilliwalla' in Hazaribagh, but in Delhi I was a thorough 'Jharkhandi'. When I returned, the city came with me too. Delhi had *defamiliarized* Hazaribagh for me.

'Give it some time,' I typed.

Besides, for Ajit, Barkattha was not far. He hadn't left the district. He could always go and see his family there.

Ajit did go to Barkattha to see his family.

He spent more days there than I had thought, and I wondered if he would ever come back. But two weeks later, I got another message from him.

'I am back! You were right. I must stay here.'

I sent him a smiley face. He sent one back.

Lake

I woke up early and saw a wide sheet of clouds spread out in the sky.

These clouds formed as puddles, each fluff separated from the other, but still clustered together. They were the altocumulus. After the dramatic cumulonimbus clouds, they are my second favourite. Altocumuli are an excellent prop for photography, so I found my camera and tiptoed out into the balcony. From there, I watched the first batch of morning walkers take to the Lake Road.

It was summer.

The time when we shut doors and windows during the day, only to open them back in the evening to let the cold air in.

In recent years, when heat simmers on the plateau, the townsmen entertain a delusion. I find people who have installed air-conditioners in their homes dismiss my concern for the rising temperature.

'Whatever you say, Mihir, there is no better place to be in summer than Hazaribagh,' they counter.

It is true.

Hazaribagh fares better in summer than its cousins

Dhanbad and Jamshedpur, sometimes Ranchi too. I give in.

'There is no better place to be in summer than Hazaribagh,' I repeat, now a party to the delusion.

I shut the door behind me, trying to make as little noise as possible, and walked down the stairs.

The sky had shed its darkness, the first mauve was trapped glowingly in the clouds above. Soon this sheet would break apart, leaving, as the day grew, only fairy trails of cirrus in the sky. Below the clouds, there was me: a lanky outline in faded trousers and t-shirt, earphones tucked in snugly, making my way to the lake. With me, there were men, women and children.

They came from all parts of the town.

From Noora, a crowd of women walked on the road. From the Collectorate, people came rushing down to Trimurti Chowk, the lake's starting point. From DVC Chowk, more arrived as disjointed streams. From Dipugarha and the northern neighbourhoods, they came along the CRPF Road.

All roads that led to the lake had woken up.

A file of policemen jogged on one side of the water. A detachment of CRPF jawans took the other. Clothes sharpened the faded air with colours, the soundscape defined by murmurs of early morning conversation.

The dawn felt soft and sympathetic on our faces.

Each morning, Hazaribagh descends to the lake to walk around the water.

The lake too puts forth its conditions. It wishes that the visitors shed their inhibitions. No pageantry happens in the morning.

Instead everyone is seen sweating, running, walking, jogging, exercising, praying, laughing, catching their breath, chatting, hugging trees, watching the water, watching birds, petting stray dogs.

Sometimes, someone finds a streetlight on and they switch it off. Sometimes, someone finds litter near the water and they take it away. So many people and groups throng to the lake. They arrive with drooping eyes, unconcerned about what they're wearing, or whether other people see them. Men come in shorts, knickers, vests, pajamas. Women come wearing loose salwar kameez, jogging pants, old saris.

The crowd mixes easily. Familiar faces are acknowledged with a nod or grin. Policemen run beside the civilians. Some, of course, *try to* run. On some days, we find a group of jawans clearing hyacinths off the water.

At the lake, morning is the time for care. One tends to unattended streetlights, notices the cleanliness. *The lake is Hazaribagh's heritage*, the backs of many concrete benches inform us. *Please keep it clean.*

Trimurti Chowk is a new name for the place. Earlier, the landmark was simply called Murti. Even before that, it was an empty space. This skewed square is named after the three merry statues assembled together to depict a tribal dance scene.

The lake's premises, its *parisar,* start with a pond at the chowk. Looking less like a part of a lake and more like an annexe, its water is sometimes clear, sometimes muddy, and always polluted.

The lake, in the town's imagination, starts properly from the Cafeteria, where it reveals its form as an assembly of three separate tanks, two large and one small.

As the first lake begins after the pond, it is also called the *beech wala*, the middle lake. It extends from the Cafeteria to the boundary walls of the Indira Gandhi Balika Vidyalaya, my Maate's former workplace. The three lakes share a border with the school, which was once a jail. Between the Cafeteria and the school, the lake supports paddle boats, fishing boats, and a motor boat on its surface.

Beneath its surface, the vegetation is visible. Water snakes pop in and out of floating leaves and grass. Small fish scatter at the slightest touch of the water. Cormorants, cranes and egrets dot the sky.

The Cafeteria too is an institution in itself.

It is contained within the larger Swarn Jayanti Park. People flock to it for myriad purposes.

The kids visit for the swings and the slides, the lovers for refuge, friends for reunions, professionals for office parties. Marriages are fixed in the park too. Prospective brides and grooms meet each other and their families over plates of dosa, paneer chilli and chowmein.

At dawn, a group of devotees occupy a small part of the park, beating drums and singing bhajans.

The garden is lined with tall eucalyptus trees facing the lake, and inside the park, neat flower beds define the walkways on both sides. A dummy giraffe, a dummy deer, and a few dummy swans inhabit the park, besides statues and real people.

Across the lake from the Cafeteria, petite bungalows of civil servants form a chain.

All the bungalows have their gardens that show in parts through nooks and gaps along their boundary walls. The height of these walls has only increased with the passing years, screening the gardens from public view.

A semicircular stage forms outside the Deputy Inspector General's residence where stands still, after all these years, a carnivorous slide.

In my childhood, I had tried several times to use it safely and failed. Its landing was broken, sharp metal erupting in wayward spikes. It has been like this forever. Today, an NTPC signboard has come up next to it, reminding passersby of the deepening work they once did at the lake and how they installed a mast-light there.

This first lake is a painter's muse.

If I were a painter, I would have made a studio here. Its angles are sharp and it does not shore. It is a indeed a tank. Trees of various kinds, from eucalyptus to date palm, surround it. Important people surround it. Sometimes I wonder if the staff working in these bungalows exchange leftover food over the walls.

The lake symbolizes power. Everything the water reflects doubles in size.

In the home improvement shows on TV, chatty experts suggest putting mirrors on walls to create an illusion of space. The lake is Hazaribagh's mirror, for the town's home improvement. It amplifies the scale of everything that comes close to it.

Like Plath's mirror, it is exact, with no preconception. When we stop caring for it, it returns to us the town's garbage.

During the 1830s, the Chhotanagpur witnessed a series of uprisings against the Company rule.

These revolts were led by the tribals in the plateau, notably the Kols and the Santhals, who grew tired of the increasing interference of the British in their lives, culture and administration. Besides, a steady influx of enterprising migrants into the plateau from Bengal and Bihar further aggravated the tensions.

These uprisings were significant events. They involved the indigenous communities standing up against a foreign, colonizing force. This chain of defiance culminated with the Santhal Rebellion of 1855–56, led by the brothers Sido and Kanhu Murmu near Dumka, some 250 kilometres from Hazaribagh. While the British were more or less able to contain these uprisings, they realized that the Chhotanagpur needed a stronger, punitive intervention. However, the lack of administrative infrastructure led people like Captain Thomas Wilkinson into strange situations.

Wilkinson was the chief planner in the quashing of the 1831 Kol Rebellion. After the job was done, he faced a dilemma. Wilkinson couldn't figure out where to put all the rebels that he had arrested. Like the other officers posted across the plateau, he accommodated them in guest houses, dak bungalows and other government buildings. But those buildings were made more for comfort and leisure, not to house convicts. Hazaribagh still wouldn't be a district until 1834.

There was no jail in the town.

The construction of a penitentiary with two wards was soon put into motion.[9]

This penitentiary, initially called the Agency Jail, was built to hold about a hundred and fifty convicts.[10] A patch of land was cleared of bushes and dug close to the proposed site to obtain building materials like clay and rocks required for construction. Consequently, all this digging left behind a crater, the first in the series.

After Hazaribagh became a district and the Company strengthened its administration, the number of native convicts in the jail grew. As demands for expansion pressed, more buildings were attached to the penitentiary. These new attachments called for another round of excavation, which not only deepened the previous crater and but also created another, the second one, next to it.

By 1852, the jail was up and functioning. It had separate wings for those who were convicted in criminal cases, those who were tried in civil cases, and the political prisoners. After the Revolt of 1857, when India became a colony of the Raj, an idea was floated in London to create special penitentiaries for European prisoners.[11] After all, the racial hierarchy, even among criminals, had to be maintained. European prisoners were to be detained preferably at hill stations, so they wouldn't evaporate under the Indian sun.

Ooty was chosen as an appropriate location in the Madras Presidency. For the presidency of Bengal, it was Hazaribagh.

In January 1862, Dr Norman Chevers, Officiating Inspector of Jails, found a spot for the new European Penitentiary. He explained the location as being close to the existing jail and situated at a little distance from Kolghatti village, on a gentle elevation.[12]

Chevers favoured this spot because it was dome-shaped. The land offered excellent drainage. Water wouldn't accumulate at the site. A thin stream separated the existing jail from Chevers' spot. He suggested putting a bridge over it and joining the two jails by a road. Chevers' recommendation was accepted. In just three years, the European Penitentiary came up close to the older jail. When the construction was finished in 1865, it left behind the third and final crater.

Both the new penitentiary and the three craters now waited to be filled.

Two narrow isthmuses join the lakes together.

The first lake in the middle is the most social, with the Cafeteria and the ghats. The second, extending northwards, is the most remote. No paved ghats exist for this one.

It starts where the Cafeteria lake ends and its catchment area also appears larger. This lake shores on two sides, while on the other two, its boundaries are sharp. A laterite road bounds the lake on the east, along which a row of date palm trees droop over the water. This lake attracts a different kind of crowd.

Towards the far end of the water, date palms release their juices into earthen pots. A small patch is cleared beneath the leaves to let the fluid ooze down and into the pots fastened round the stem to collect each drop. Before sunrise, the liquid is a health drink. After the sun heats it up, it turns alcoholic. There are several admirers of this drink, in both its forms. Those who take it before sunrise say it boosts their energy. The intoxicated men, on the other hand, are found blissful under the trees.

Across the water, shines the white facade of the Jail Superintendent's residence. I find this bungalow to be the most *value-for-designation* property, since besides the house, its gardens roll gently into the lake.

In persistent summers, when the water shrinks, the exposed land develops cracks, creating the illusion of being parched.

A few years ago, one evening in May, I walked up to this lake's end. A small barrier stopped the water from flowing into the depression below. Along the check dam, I saw that the land looked rather dry and ready for walking. I had come to this lake after walking around the first one. The summer heat was present, but more than the heat, I was irritated by the humidity which the lake lent to the air. All the walking had left me tired, and soon I was wishing to get back home. I looked at the parched shore again and reasoned that if the ground held my weight, I would be able to take a shortcut.

The walk started out fine.

The ground was wobbly near the water, so I decided not to stray there. I kept as much distance as possible between myself and the water, and was able to cover more than half of the route. I crossed the Jail Superintendent's rolling gardens, and when I looked back at the laterite road across the water, the palm trees had shrunk.

The road towards home appeared before me. It was the final stretch. I would walk around the edge of the lake and climb up the elevation to get to the road. If I made it, I would be home within minutes.

I took one step.

The earth shook a little under my weight, but it held me up. I took the next step and the universe collapsed.

I dropped instantly into a thick, black, viscous sludge. Knees down, I was stuck, drawn slowly into the bog. I had read before that if you struggle in a marsh, it pulls you in faster. When I realized I was half-buried in the sludge, I became totally still. A tiny awareness of the muddy mass shifting beneath me grew in my mind. I wasn't imagining it. The sludge was indeed moving. It was slow and measured, but it was shifting. I felt that I was sinking too.

Luckily, I spotted an ipomoea plant nearby. It offered one of its long, thetthar arms and I grabbed it tightly, pulling myself closer to the land. My body cut through the sludge like a knife, smoothly, but my mind at the time was a tornado. When I emerged from the bog, I was one colour from the waist up and another waist down. A two-in-one combo.

Embarrassed, I walked home, hoping that no one saw me. Before entering the house, I washed the mud off at the colony hand pump. I never attempted walking on any dry-looking lake again.

Still, I like this lake more than the first.

Few people crowd the water here and the surroundings too are placid. Very few cars enter the laterite road, and the people who come to sit by the lake, do so in silence. Sometimes they come with cigarettes, sometimes with a drink.

When *sanskaari* townsmen look at this lake, they regard it with aversion. It has amassed a shady reputation over the years. So many people have drowned in its water, so many murdered bodies have appeared, bloated, on its surface. Ghosts flit like fireflies over this lake. It is a source of legends, speculations. Some say, secret passageways run below the water. They all lead to the jail. Some say there exist underground wells.

If you are swallowed by one, you will never return.

The lake comes with its lore, the water prefabricated for imagination. Near the shore, it sprouts crimson lotuses.

On July 6, 1832, a boy was born in Ireland's Down county.

I have worked hard to find him.

His name was John.

John grew up in Belfast. He attended elementary school in the city and later studied medicine at the Queen's University. Soon after finishing college and at the age of twenty-four, he arrived in India.

John entered the country as a doctor, but only a year after his arrival, the revolt of 1857 broke out. A civil servant at the time, John found himself attached to the service of the Rattray's Sikhs, who were deployed in Bihar. By September 1857, they had 'secured' Ara and also Gaya. The Sikhs, under the command of Captain Thomas Rattray, were also instrumental in suppressing the rebellion in Hazaribagh.

A curious, red building at the DVC Chowk near the lake, often called the Lal Kothi and which currently functions as the Damodar Valley Corporation's Accounts Office in Hazaribagh, housed anywhere between a hundred and fifty to two hundred soldiers of the Rattray's Sikhs. On one of the windows, intricate woodwork draws attention towards the central feature, a shield with five kirpans, daggers embedded over it.

In 2015, I met James Rattray, the great-grandson of Captain Thomas Rattray, in Scotland. On a rainy Sunday, he drove two hours from his home in Perthshire to pick me up from Bridge of Allan. On the way, I showed him the location of Hazaribagh on a map along with a few photographs of the red building, which historians have called Rattray House.

'Named after your great-grandfather's battalion, this building.'

James, forty years my elder, had lived much of his life in South Africa and only recently returned to Scotland. Like myself, he was also starting to understand his town's local history. When we reached his home at Killiecrankie after crossing a portion of the Cairngorms National Park, all rain and black heather, he showed me Thomas' old notes, his diary, some of his paintings and sketches. Reading his accounts, I realized that Thomas never actually came to Hazaribagh. The soldiers had come to the town on his orders, while he had to stay back in Gaya.

After a hearty lunch and my unseemly attempts at trying the Scottish kilt, James drove me back to Bridge of Allan. Five years on, we remain good friends.

But I was talking about John. John from Ireland. In 1857.

After the mutiny was over, John resumed his regular duties and was posted in Bihar's Champaran as the district's

Civil Surgeon. From Champaran, he went to serve briefly in Odisha's Cuttack, and in 1866, John arrived in Hazaribagh as the town's Jail Superintendent. In Hazaribagh, besides the congenial climate, he was greeted by three massive craters, red wounds gaping on the surface of earth, awaiting a facelift.

It was during his tenure in Hazaribagh that John landscaped the craters into lakes. Earlier, whatever water was found in the pits was left over from the monsoon rains. The craters were merely shallow ponds, their water muddy, the sludge thick at the bottom. A permanent feeding source was required to effectively turn the ponds into lakes.

Fortunately for John, the craters were dug near a topographical depression occurring along the route of a prehistoric river. During monsoon and along this riverine route, small streams originating from the higher villages of Noora and Kolghatti flowed down into the craters. Local historian and megalithic researcher, Subhashis Das, told me about this lost river when I met him at his home. He expertly charted this river's route right up to the Siwane river that flows north of Hazaribagh. John engineered these streams in such a manner that they emptied their waters into the boggy ponds. To hold this water in, John built a barrier, a check dam, on the last crater. When monsoon arrived the next year, the rain, along with the flooding streams, pushed the water levels up. John also schemed the lakes in a way that water from one crater flowed into the other. No two water bodies were on the same elevation, the lakes were fashioned as steps.

It must have taken years for the craters to fill up and

for the lakes to take their present form. When John left Hazaribagh, the site was still a work-in-progress. I am not sure if he ever returned to see his enterprise attain its beautiful fruition.

I found John as a stray reference in one Eyre Chatterton's 1901 book, *The Story of Fifty Years' Mission Work in Chhota Nagpur.*[13]

Chatterton was a Catholic priest with the Dublin Mission. Like John, he was also from Ireland. Chatterton's book is primarily concerned with describing the work of the Mission across various Chhotanagpur towns. However, when he wrote about Hazaribagh, he also gave a brief history of the place. It was in those pages that he recounted the experience of seeing the lakes. Chatterton saw only two lakes, missing perhaps the smallest one on the west, as most people are prone to, but he did mention that the lakes in Hazaribagh 'added considerably to its beauty.'

Unfortunately, John did not live to read Chatterton's appraisal of his work.

Six years before Chatterton published his book, Brigade Surgeon Lieutenant Colonel John Martin Coates, MD, FCU, suffered a heart attack and died in Calcutta. John's last professional engagement was as the Principal of Calcutta Medical College. In 2019, I was able to locate Ms. Noeline Cole, a relative of John who lives in New Zealand. She was as thrilled to receive my email as I was to receive her reply. 'He seemed to be an amazing man,' she wrote to me, after I had explained the connection between John and the lakes of Hazaribagh. It certainly appears that John was an amazing man. An obituary published in the *Indian Medical*

Gazette in 1895 quoted an extract from a letter sent by one of John's Indian friends.

'It will be very difficult now at this hard time to replace him.'

History is such an incredible thing.

To think that the origin of the lake is tied inextricably to a history of punishment, repression and violence feels unimaginable today. Surely, it weren't the Europeans who laboured and dug the earth to build the jails, and surely, it weren't the Europeans who toiled in the gardens to create Hazaribagh's lovely charm. It is more likely that the native convicts, among whom several were tribals, were coerced into beauty's craftsmanship. When we look at beauty, we also look at its history, and in postcolonial countries like India, this history is marred with violence, upon body, land *and* identity.

In 2020, an old tank that was constructed by Major Simpson, also a former DC of Hazaribagh and under whose supervision the 1857 revolt was 'contained' in the district, was given a facelift. A pleasant park was added to the pond too. In the end, the site was named 'Simpson Park'. Immediately, a stiff opposition was registered by the townsmen over the park's name and it forced the authorities to change its name to the neutral 'Zila Parishad Park'. The history of the lake which I have offered is the history of a land's colonisation. It is one narrative. But a different narrative is building too, one that recognises that history is not objective, and through that recognition, strives not to erase the event but revise and reclaim it. Through time, the jails and the lakes have grown detached from each other, one standing for punishment, the other for the picturesque, both developing in the process their own separate narratives.

The European penitentiary was abolished in 1882, after the government decided that British prisoners living in Indian jails were better off in the different islands under their control. Australia was one such island. After its abolition, the building was converted into a reformatory for juvenile offenders.[14]

For a hundred years, that building functioned as a reformatory. The lakes too became clearer, settling all sediments and secrets deeper under the water.

In 1983, the Bihar government sent one of its teachers from the famous Netarhat Vidyalaya to Hazaribagh. A teacher of Physics, this man was tasked with transforming the reformatory into a residential school for girls.

The symbolism of little girls living in a jail could not be more stark.

This Physics teacher was Shriman BD Pandey. His colleagues and students called him *Shrimanji*. This was one of the traditions he had brought with him from Netarhat. In the January of 1984, Shrimanji was appointed the first principal of the Indira Gandhi Balika Vidyalaya.

My newly-married Maate came to Hazaribagh a year after the school's foundation. Travelling for the first time to the plateau from Bihar, she remembers how the vermillion on her head had completely soiled her father's white clothes.

She joined the school as a Sanskrit teacher, also living for the first six years inside campus as a hostel warden. When I ask her about the past, she says that it was impossible for her to drive nails into the walls.

'Nothing could go through those British walls.'

When she lived on campus, she also witnessed strange happenings.

'Big rocks would fly into our rooms.

It was scary because as the warden, I knew that there was no girl loitering outside at such a late hour. After all, I was the one who did the nightly roll-call.

Often the lights would play with me too.'

Around 1987-88, the construction of the teachers' quarters had commenced nearby. The site chosen for these quarters, which we would later know as 'Teachers Colony' was located near Dr Chevers' proposed bridge, on the stretch of land that lay between the two jails.

In 1991, three buildings, each housing four apartments were ready. I was born the same year. Maate moved into her new home with me.

A good enough walk with all these stories, I hope. It is still morning, the clouds are still there in the sky, the people also are still very much present by the lake.

I returned after walking only half the circuit, leaving the rest for the evening. On the way, I stopped at a few places to take photos. One would go to Facebook, another on Instagram. Like me, many people were returning to their respective homes too, but I had comfortably zoned out from the crowd.

The sun was no longer timid. Light, trees, the shadows; I watched the chiaroscuro dance over the tar road.

It was summer, after all, and the morning had advanced swiftly.

Road and railway bridges over Tilaiya Dam's reservoir with Hazaribagh district on the left and Koderma on the right

Top: Canary Hill and the bypass road • *Bottom:* Sunset at Hazaribagh Lake

Top: Salparni Waterfall in monsoon • *Bottom:* The dilapidated watchtower at Harhad Forest overlooking the dry Muhane River

Top: Forest Rest House at Rajderva, Hazaribagh Wildlife Sanctuary
Bottom: Paddy fields in Karanpura Valley at Keredari

Top: Gittikocha Waterfall in monsoon • *Bottom:* Forest and river in the southern escarpment near Barkagaon

Top: Raja Talab at Jorakath Hill Village • *Bottom (left and right):* Bokaro River near Pindra with Lugu Buru on the left and Jhumra Pahad on the right

Top: Rock formation by Bokaro River near Tapin

Sal trees in summer along Morangi-Churchu Road

It is the smallest, the third lake. Again, an isthmus separates it from the first.

Most of the time, the water is screened by what we call *jalkumbhi*, the water hyacinths. It forms the breeding grounds for birds and is an eyesore for humans.

When the administration clears the weeds, the birders and avifauna conservationists feel uneasy. When the weeds are left unattended, the townsmen make a face. This little, square lake terminates on the west against a decrepit road, beyond which Jheel Nagar and the villages of Kolghatti and Noora begin. The high walls of my Maate's school appear even higher from here.

The easterly breeze starts from the water and travels to its larger counterparts. During monsoon, this lake inundates first, sending the excess water down an aqueduct into the middle lake. When the middle lake brims over, it sends the surplus to the next.

John's decision to put the lakes on different elevations works well today, as water flowing from one lake to the other keeps the cluster alive.

In the evening, photographers from the town, with professional as well as phone cameras, assemble to shoot the sunset.

Students arrive on scooters with friends.

Evening walkers stay on their course.

Tourists keep close to the boating stall.

At Trimurti Chowk, mobile eateries pop up to cater to the visitors. Tandoori Chai is now a staple. 'No less than the Khan Market of Delhi,' I quip, to myself. On the ghats, vendors selling lemon tea canvass the territory for potential customers. When luck permits, I find a group of men jamming to the chords of a guitar.

The lake parisar extends over a hundred acres.

At Cafeteria, people who come from far off places in the district splurge money. The toy train, the Swarn Jayanti Express, makes five small rounds in the garden. Students who study elsewhere return to the lake for reunions. There is space for everyone. If not this lake, then that lake. If not that lake, then the one beside that.

The lovestrucks and lovelorns hold their hearts out for exhibition. Some exhibit their Mahindra Thars.

When I walk around the lake in the evening, I too feel the urge to bring my heart to the same degree of exhibition, but I am often fearful. I do not allow the vulnerability. 'Someday, just someday,' I tell myself as if this was all a movie, 'I will also find love by this lake.'

These lakes are a product of experiments. People have a tendency to do things to them. The most recent addition is the Gandhi Statue. It sits half-heartedly, questioning its own existence, in the smallest lake.

The nation's father is given a remarkably sculpted upper body, so whenever one looks at him, it seems as if Gandhiji has only just returned from the gym. A hurriedly devised mud path goes to the base of the statue, from where a cheap steel staircase takes the visitor up to the observation deck. On the deck, a flimsy railing is meant to stop people from falling into the water below. I haven't seen people falling yet, but the railing sure has drooped.

The lake sustains extreme ideas.

Sometimes, when the administration is generous, statues

of dwarf elephants and gods appear, floating on the water, and the spectacle brings much thrill. A mandatory fountain seems to glide over the water, erupting on *extremely* important occasions, shooting jets of water *into* the water.

Sometimes, some of the ghats get tiled. Some other ghats get marbled. Some unfortunate ghats make do with concrete work only. Either the money runs out or the contractor. The case of *thekedaar bhaag gaya* occurs often.

Some deepening work happens at one corner, some excavation takes place at another corner. Newer constructions often wake the northern lake from its quiet slumber to make it perform its initial utility of being a mud mine. The date palm trees existing on the shore are spared, but the ground around them is excavated.

Today, these trees can be seen rising from small pyramids that exist in tablets of water. One of my friends has termed these pyramids Hazaribagh's imminent archaeological wonder. Administrative power comes sugar-charged to test one idea after another at the lake, all in the name of *sundarikaran*, the administrators themselves compensating for all the experiments they couldn't do in school laboratories. Besides, if the many residences along the Lake Road are any indication, there is no dearth of powerful people living by the water.

Some bureaucrat adds X feature to the lake and they are transferred. The person who arrives next adds Y feature to the lake and they are transferred too. We watch and judge the latest developments, reminding ourselves that the lake is still writing itself, that this chapter is not yet finished.

On January 25, 1996, Maate and I were returning from Begusarai in Bihar. We had gone to visit Maate's father—my nanaji—and stay at his kothi for some days. At nanaji's kothi, Maate and I were supposed to participate in a havan administered by him. The havan was meant to bring us peace, good alliances, and luck.

Most of the night service buses from Begusarai terminated in Ranchi. Hazaribagh, when the roads were rough and narrow, arrived three to four hours before dawn. We were in one such bus. It would pass through Hazaribagh at around two in the night.

My Maate, being practical, decided that we should remain at the bus stand, maybe at one of the dhabas, and wait for the sun to come up. It was a sensible plan. We were one woman and a child, and the lake area was then notorious for crime. The bus stand was never deserted, there was always some commotion. Maate reckoned it was the safest option. Besides, even if we wanted to go home, the rickshawallahs wouldn't agree.

Maate would say, the hours between midnight and three were the hours of the paranormal. Ghosts, *pishachs*, *dayans* and *chudails* roamed free in the dark, looking for prey.

When the bus stopped at the stand, it was two on the dot. A gentleman alighted with us. Maate asked him if he too was planning to stay at the bus stand.

'I live close to Columba's College, madam,' he said. 'I will walk. It will only take me fifteen minutes.'

After he left, Maate grabbed my hand and we walked towards the nearest dhaba.

Then, like an apparition, a rickshaw appeared. It steered

close to us and stopped. As if in a trance, Maate uttered, '*Chaloge*?'

She could not make out the face of the rickshawallah. But she wasn't too concerned about it. In January, the cold in Hazaribagh is biting. We were busy shivering, adjusting our sweaters, jackets, caps and scarves for maximum protection. '*Haan*,' the man replied. 'Where to?'

'*Jheel par*' Maate answered.

The rickshawallah would take twenty rupees. It was reasonable fare. There was no haggling involved.

To reach home, we needed to cross seven stretches of road. The first stretch was from the bus stand to the District Board Chowk, the second from the District Board Chowk to the Collectorate Gate, the third from the Collectorate Gate to the present Trimurti Chowk, the fourth along the middle lake, the fifth was the isthmus leading to Maate's school, the sixth was the jail road with Dr Chevers' bridge, and finally, the seventh was the colony road to our quarters.

The first two stretches passed quickly.

Maate was occupied with fixing the luggage against the rickshaw's hood. By this time, I was also sufficiently layered against the cold.

The third stretch followed a downward slope to the lake, passing the Zila School. From this point onwards, Maate had nothing to do. The sky was clear, the stars were shining. She doesn't remember the moon. From her seat, she could see that the rickshawallah's trousers were folded up to his shins. From his silhouette, it seemed like he was fairly young.

The rickshaw wheeled down the slope, the chill rising. It was only going to get colder, as we were now approaching the lake. The fourth stretch of road ran along its length.

Once at the lake, we had effectively left the town behind. From here, the chances of seeing another person were less than that of spotting a hyena or a jackal. There were plenty of jackals around at that time. Whenever they howled, it would pierce the chilling quiet of the night. We were not that scared of their howling, it was quite routine for us. We were, however, scared of the *pagli ghanti*, the jail alarm. It has rung only twice, at least in my memory. The ringing of the *pagli ghanti* meant that a prisoner had escaped. In such an event, we were supposed to close the doors, shut the windows. We were not to go anywhere for a good couple of hours.

It was the rickshawallah who broke the silence. He was speaking astronomy.

'These stars in the sky... the constellations... it's all *Akashganga*, the Milky Way, you know?'

Maate, who initially thought he was blabbering, was drawn in by the sudden interpellation. Still, she thought the man was talking more to himself than to her.

'You are seeing the stars, madam, aren't you?' the rickshawallah asked again, a bit louder this time.

Maate couldn't ignore the question this time.

'Yes, yes,' she replied.

Maate thought the rickshawallah was well-educated, maybe a college student. His voice was respectful. It couldn't hurt to strike up a conversation.

'*Toh rickshawale*, tell me, do you study?'

'*Nahi*, madam,' he replied.

'Not in the day?' Maate pressed.

There was a moment of silence, before the rickshawallah said curtly, 'I cannot study in the day.'

Maate reasoned that maybe he didn't have enough money. Maybe he did double-shifts with his rickshaw. The lake went quiet again. Crickets heightened their shrill racket. In the darkness, the tricycle moved. Maate noticed that throughout the ride, not once did she experience any jerk on the road. It was as if we were flying, levitating half an inch above the ground.

On the isthmus, we were in the middle of the two lakes. The Cafeteria lake was on our left, the northern one on the right. On the shore of the northern lake was the Jail Superintendent's residence. Maate saw a faint light emanating from the campus. As if reading her mind, the rickshawallah asked, 'Do you you know what that bungalow is, madam?'

Maate was of course familiar with the place in question.

'*Haan*! I know what that is. The Jail Superintendent lives there.'

Maate felt accomplished at her reply, as if answering correctly had earned her validation from the young rickshawallah, who, by his very own admission, did not, or could not, study.

'I was here the other day. The day before yesterday, actually,' the rickshawallah began.

'There were others too. Netaji was with us. We had assembled to talk about our plans.'

Maate was dumbstruck.

'Netaji...' she mouthed the word in surprise.

'Yes, Netaji Bose, madam. He was with us. We had assembled to discuss plans, what the Azad Hind Fauj should do next. There aren't many of us left now.'

Maate's head was spinning.

The day before yesterday was January 23. It was

Subhash Chandra Bose Jayanti, Netaji's birthday. She tried to compose her thoughts, but at that very moment, the rickshawallah said something even more terrifying.

'*Aapko darr toh nahi lag raha hai na*? You're not getting scared now, madam, are you?' he asked calmly, without betraying any emotion.

Whatever Maate was thinking at the moment, she still did not believe that the man could be a ghost.

She thought he was probably insane and she cursed herself for being in this situation. *Vinashkale viprit buddhi*! Should have remained at the bus stand, she thought.

His question, however, was still hanging.

'No,' she recollected herself, 'why should I be scared?'

The rickshawallah said nothing.

The dark lake fell into silence again, the water black like a void.

We passed the school gate and turned towards the jail. Maate could now see the lights coming from our quarters in the colony. One more road and it would all be over. We were still flying, the wheels not once rattling or rolling into a ditch. Maate reasoned that it must be the man's driving. It was crucial for her to rationalize the events that were unfolding before our eyes at that time. The colony road would arrive shortly. She was on the edge of her seat.

Without glancing back even once, the rickshawallah read her again. '*Aapko sach me darr toh nahi lag raha na*, madam?' Clearly, he was in control.

Maate replied again in the negative, as the rickshaw turned sharply towards the colony. By this time, she had started planning our escape.

The colony road was an upward incline, and almost all rickshawallahs had to get down from their seat to drag the carriage up on foot. This man did nothing of the sort. Even before Maate could formulate any exit strategies, the rickshaw stopped at the first building in the colony. We had arrived. Maate had not told him which building among the three was ours.

Our house was on the first floor.

When we stepped down from the rickshaw, Maate made sure to ensure my safety. I was half-asleep. I had seen nothing, heard nothing. Resting my head sideways on her knees, I had slept the whole time.

Maate ordered me to take the key upstairs and unlock the door.

'I will come after you with the luggage. Go!'

The rickshawallah stood close, not saying anything.

Maate then unloaded the luggage, holding the bags in both her hands. 'Wait here,' she told the rickshawallah. 'I will come back and pay you.'

I went upstairs and unlocked the door. Maate followed. After I was inside the house, along with the luggage, she bolted the door from outside and went back down the stairs to pay him.

When Maate emerged from the building, the road was empty. There was no one in sight. There was no sound of a rickshaw leaving. No tyre buzzed against the tarmac. No chain struggled against the iron bar. There was no screech of metallic friction penetrating the night.

There were no signs of an empty carriage being driven away in the dark.

Forest

When winter retreats from the plateau, the forest changes its colour.

Once the days grow longer, the sun gathers its heat and pours it little by little over the sal trees. The green leaves age, become loose at the branches, and by February, they turn yellow and fall to the ground. This fall endures for hours, like a chain reaction, and in the forest, leaves are shed in an uninterrupted sequence. The slightest touch of a wind can initiate the fall.

On the many forest roads, trails and walkways, the spectacle of leaves falling lazily from the trees creates an immaculate dreamscape.

There are many forests in and around the plateau. Except for the small patch at Canary Hill, the rest exist along the escarpment.

The plateau itself is a smudged circle, the forest surrounding the town in a protective fence. The trees tame hot air from the plains and send to us colder winds. They trap and release moisture in the air, giving us the rains.

When rain batters the table-top, water tumbles down from the highland, rushing from all sides to the lower plateau below. Each drop is a packet of energy. They combine together to erode the ground. The water cleaves the land into gullies and gulches. So urgent is its motion that hardly anything is retained by the town.

Monsoon after monsoon, the gullies are renewed, reinforced into riverine paths. Five major rivers originate from the plateau as thin streams. These rivers are Siwane, Konar, Barakar, Bokaro and Muhane. They are infants in the town which battles water shortage in summer. When the monsoon recedes, the rivers grow malnourished with the passing months, disappearing ultimately into the ground under the summer's heat.

When the water disappears, it leaves irregular, dark traces on the sand.

If the five rivers are juvenile in the town, they hit adolescence at the escarpment. In the forest, they are joined by stray streams that too are activated on the plateau. Gullies widen into valleys. Eroding the topsoil, the rivers reveal the rocks underneath. The water passes through tests which boulders put up for it. Sometimes, the current is strong, and the water splits the hill to make way for itself. Sometimes, the terrain is rough and steep, and the rivers fall down into the valley below. This is a shortcut, and by taking such shortcuts, the rivers create waterfalls. Throughout the escarpment, there are scattered a number of waterfalls. They occur as plunge falls, snake falls, cascades and water-steps. They are tall and short, narrow and wide, impressive and unimpressive. Most of them carry water only for six to eight months of the year.

When I started walking in the forest, the first gift I

received was that of sleep. Months after I had left Delhi, the mind had acknowledged depression as a persistent presence.

It was just that: presence, an unquantifiable abstraction.

I hadn't wished or willed it away, but I was paying it less attention. In the forest and with water, I could forget it easily, at least momentarily. Though sleep often remained elusive, I soon understood that the forest held a cheat code. Walking up and down the hills, taking trails into isolated zones, following a stream down to its fall would tire me so much that by the time I returned home, the body longed only for bed.

I think of the plateau's forests in the singular because they are connected, even if separated physically by roads, railways and rivers, and notionally by the forest department boundaries. The forest itself does not follow a uniform code.

On the highland, it starts as scrub, followed by the open sal forest with low undergrowth. In the moist, valley regions, it grows into a mixed woodland. The more sheltered the forest gets, the more depth it acquires. It grows denser along the slopes of the escarpment.

Before the plateau merges with the lower country below, the rivers begin to negotiate their width with the hills. The water system becomes richer and nuanced, supporting a variety of life besides the tall sal trees.

Wading into this forest is a task. The feet need to be careful and precise, hands aware of thorns on the twigs. Cuts and gashes are more frequent here. Us humans occupy the higher and the lower spaces, everything in between is the forest.

Elephants arrive too.

The herd enters from the south-west in Barkagaon. It then moves along the foot of the plateau towards Charhi. If they are conscious of the forest and do not stray, they pass. If they lose the cover, they are found fallen in coal mines. Sometimes, unbeknownst to elephants, the forest shrinks, and they return the next year to find themselves in the open. Sometimes, development happens, and they return the next year to find their green corridor replaced by a railway track.

From Charhi, the herd keeps to the forest and reaches Gomia. When the elephants march out, they follow the forest of the Konar basin, finding shelter in the northern and eastern escarpments. Here the herd branches out.

The first group takes the forest straight to Bagodar, while the second makes a detour. It travels up the elevation and skirts round Jhumra Pahad. Following a narrow strip of forest, it crosses NH 100 at Banhe and arrives near the villages of Khaira and Simradabh. These villages mark the end of the highland. When the elephants leave the plateau, they emerge on the Grand Trunk Road at Gorhar, from where they travel northwards to Chalkusha.

Elephants normally do not come up to the town, but in 2013, a lost herd had somehow strayed into the Canary Hill forest. Work on the new road had not started then. I was studying in Delhi. I read later on the internet that they found their way out through Jabra forest, but not before damaging a portion of Gibraltar.

Against the assault of rapid urbanization and the resulting loss of the plateau's forest cover, there exists a pause twenty kilometres from the town. It appears as an uninterrupted stretch of woodland. We call it the 'national park'.

Hazaribagh National Park is a misnomer. The place is a myth. It does not exist, it has never legally existed.

In 1955, an impassioned plan was made by the forest officer, SP Shahi, to turn this stretch of forest into a national park, but his efforts did not yield a legal notification. From 1955 to 1976, the forest was a national park with no official backing.

In his essay 'Battling for Wildlife in Bihar', which appears in Valmik Thapar's anthology *Saving Wild Tigers*, Shahi recounts the frustrating and often hilarious workings of the bureaucracy at Bihar's forest department. It was the corrupt system, flavoured with a chain of short-lived governments and garnished liberally with a series of administrative mood-swings that posed the gravest challenge to procuring an executive order for the forest.

For twenty years the woods were a national park. For twenty years, they were not. The forest road was ready, the pamphlets advertised the tract as a national park, the tourists came and went away. All of this happened while the file was pushed from one forest minister to the next.

Finally, in 1976, the forest was notified as a wildlife sanctuary, this time with legal backing, and this is what the jungle is today.

Fiction and fact create a variegated system of knowledge.

Because in its initial decades, the forest was known as a national park, the phrase has quietly seeped into the town's vocabulary too. It now occupies a respected spot in Hazaribagh's list of tourist attractions. The place's imagination is incomplete without its national park.

It does not matter that the forest is officially a sanctuary, and that national parks are, technically, different legal entities. The enduring idea of this forest as a national park is so strong that the phrase *Hazaribagh Wildlife Sanctuary* appears only on the entry gates. 'Tell the truth but tell it slant,' said Emily Dickinson. The forest still is a national park for us. There is even a Wikipedia page for this fine work of mythology.

From 2011 to 2014, I was searching in my hometown a tourist destination. As a literature student fascinated with irony, I echoed one of Jane Austen's most enduring lines, convinced it was a truth universally acknowledged that an Indian land in possession of good forest must be in want of a tourist destination tag.

At the same time, the government in Delhi was also convinced that an Indian land in possession of good forest must be in want of mines. That the mines emerged as winners is a fact more apparent today than it was at the time. In 2011, I simply did not care.

I had found my first waterfall in the national park's Salparni forest.

Salparni translates to 'leaves of sal trees'.

Earlier, whenever Maate took me there, we would go straight to the small lake inside. We would spend half an hour gazing at the water, and return. When the Alto wasn't around, Maate hired cars. When there were more people, she hired jeeps.

Maate's love for travel is my most profound inheritance.

Neither of us was heavily deterred by the Naxalis in the forest, though this did not mean that we weren't careful. At dusk, we knew it was time to return. Even in the daytime, access was limited. In the evening, it was better to be with the lake in Hazaribagh than in the forest outside.

Maate stuck to roads, they were her threshold. Beyond roads, we wouldn't go. The hills with no roads were for me secret places, demanding exploration. The hills with no roads were for her dangerous places, demanding seclusion.

As long as I was a child, Maate and I travelled across the plateau with caution. When I turned eighteen and the Alto came along, I morphed my vacations into drives to the forest. When the Delhi 'bros' were going to Kasol, this Hazaribagh bro would be walking in a random forest. I did mostly stick to the roads, the habit would not go away. But slowly, I was also making my own roads into the woods.

As long as I was on a path, whether it was made by myself before or someone else, I would be fine.

In the October of 2011, the sky was a crisp blue. I remember there were no clouds. My relatives from Muzaffarpur had come to spend a week with us. It being a Sunday, we decided to go to Salparni. My Muzaffarpur folks are Hazaribagh's most loyal tourists. With time, the family has expanded to four generations. My four cousins are married with kids, but this growing tree has managed to extend one sinuous root, three hundred kilometres away, into Hazaribagh. The plateau for them is their second home.

At the time we drove to the forest, the Muzaffarpur group consisted of my Mausima, my Mausaji and Mitthoo didi. Even before they had arrived in Hazaribagh, I was already speaking with Maate about the possibility of a waterfall at Salparni.

'The land there is so *up and down*—water must fall *somewhere.*'

I was beginning to notice the geography, making assumptions and conjectures about streams and rivers.

As I was trained in literature, I knew the words *context, critique* and *problematic*. I did not know the words *topography, terrain* and *undulation*. The land for me was still *up and down*.

At Salparni, we went to the lake first.

The waterfall must be somewhere in the forest, I thought. While we appreciated the sal trees and the water, I was desperate to go deeper. On our way to the lake, we had passed a tri-junction. A forest road shot due east from there. We had not taken that road before. Maate always maintained that it only went further into the forest. There was just jungle and nothing much to see. This time, I didn't want to take her word for it.

Near the lake, there was the defunct forest rest house and its pale dining room. A framed, faded and frayed poster on one of the dining room walls had a tiger drinking from a pool of water. The photo was captioned *Project Tiger*. Our national park was never a part of that project. I was amused by the irrelevance of that morose poster in Salparni. Maybe some forest officer had installed it years ago out of love, because, *why not*? It seemed like a similar case with the empty rest house too. It was constructed to house fairies and ghosts, because, *why not*?

The dining room was dingy and unpleasant. The

furniture was delicate, the ceiling home to spiders. Outside the dining room, I met Akbar *ji*. He was then the caretaker of the rest house.

'Sir, *koi jharna hai idhar*?' I asked him, inquiring if there was a waterfall in the forest. He confirmed that there was.

I would need to take the other road from the tri-junction to get there.

'*Dekhiyega thoda*, the bridge is broken,' Akbar *ji* added.

I asked him if he could accompany us to the fall, but since there was no one else to stay by the rest house, he refused. It was a fair excuse. We left Akbar *ji* at the lake, and following his directions, set out to find the waterfall.

We arrived at the broken bridge after driving through the other tri-junction road for some time.

Because it was a path I had never taken before, the excitement to see what it offered was high. The same sal trees looked different, the same shrubs and bushes appeared new. I was eager to create signification, attach meanings to everything I saw. We had never seen much wildlife on the road to the lake. On this road, however, I sensed a silly hope building inside the car of seeing, if not a tiger, then perhaps a spotted deer or a fox. What we saw instead were cows, their bells tinkling amidst the trees. We did not see any deer, not even a porcupine. Eight years later, in 2019, I would startle a herd of spotted deer on the same road.

I parked the car before the bridge. As we walked towards it, I spotted a large, gaping hole in the middle of the cement structure. A shallow river flowed under it. I saw the water rushing north. Akbar *ji* had told me that the waterfall was close to the bridge, but we hadn't yet heard the sound of water falling.

Waterfalls are usually first heard and then seen. It is this sensory sequence which spurs the imagination and later completes the experience. After we walked past the bridge, I found a forest trail going into the bushes. Both the water and the trail went in the same direction.

Maate was hesitant at first.

'*Saanp-bichhoo hoga udhar*,' she said, fearing venomous reptiles.

I coaxed her into following me for some time.

'If we find nothing, we will just come back,' I reasoned.

My Gangetic Plains relatives were thrilled to be in the forest. I could make them walk for hours and they wouldn't complain. They were as eager to find the waterfall as I was. Maate relented.

Though the undergrowth was annoying, the trail was still prominent on the ground. The first person to reach the end of it was Mitthoo didi. She saw the view open in front of her, turned towards me, and said, 'Wow!' I reached second. I saw the view, turned towards the elders, and said, 'Wow!' This went on for a bit, till all of us had assembled in front of the falling water.

The stream under the bridge had reached the top of the fall. It condensed into a narrow channel and made the first drop from the extreme left. The first stage of rocks mellowed it into a pool large enough for a person to swim in. From the pool, the water pushed down another rocky outcrop which sliced it into two streams. The first stream remained on the left, its clear water shining under the sun, while the second trailed off to the right, coating gentler sheets of rock with a kinetic, glossy film. The former dropped again, creating a second pool, while the latter collected into a third adjacent to it. When these streams reached the bottom, they met in the final, largest pool. After that, it was one stream again.

There was no one else in the forest that day. The waterfall was all ours.

We started climbing down the rocks. It was easy because they formed giant steps. When we reached the bottom, we cautiously edged past the pool. Then, we chose our preferred spots and sat down.

There was purity in the environment and we were its exclusive beneficiaries. The water had ceased to be merely a sound and was now a mature sight. My relatives were ecstatic. Mitthoo didi was seeing a waterfall for the first time in her life. The rest of us, though familiar with waterfalls elsewhere, were seeing a waterfall in Hazaribagh for the first time. It looked unreal for the everyday which was Hazaribagh, for us. It *felt* unreal. The forest felt unreal, and so did the little sounds and noises that surrounded us. The sound of water falling was therapeutic. Some distance away and facing us was a lone watchtower, its structure impressive, white against the green foliage.

Maate and Mausima found a splendid arch created by some spindly shoots by the stream. They masqueraded as Radha and Krishna under it. A site of *Sringar Rasa* for the Sanskrit teacher in her, Maate took to the waterfall easily. Half an hour ago that day, she wouldn't let anyone walk on the forest trail. But today, over the following years, the waterfall has become a familiar as well as a familial place for her.

The pool was too inviting for Mausaji and me. I climbed

back up and rushed to the Alto for a couple of long towels that served as the car's seat covers. We spent about an hour with the waterfall, and after saturation, returned home.

The waterfall at Salparni was my first. Some romance has grown into it. I feel protective about it. I get enraged when I see it covered with litter after a stupid picnic or a polluting '*vanbhoj*'. Sometimes, I clear it off the rubbish. Sometimes, friends join me. When the cleaning is done, we bring the garbage to the city for disposal. If the holding sacks fall short in number, we assemble the trash in a corner. But it is also true that sometimes I just don't bother. *Kachra hai toh hai*. If nobody else is bothered why should I be the only cleaner?

I have seen the waterfall comatose in summer and thunder in monsoon. I have enjoyed its soulful company in autumn, and I have shown it to, or rather shared it with, people I love.

Poets are such prosaic lovers.

Words turn against us when we fall in love. Talent lodges itself, useless, against love's glare. Articulation evades the alphabet. You *see* me when I show you my waterfalls. I mean it without innuendo, though not necessarily without flirtation. *I will show you mine if you show me yours.* Take me to your forest and I will take you to mine. Give me your rocks and I will build you a cairn. Show me your sand and I will show you a river.

Sometimes, I go to the waterfall without a reason, and in my affinity for it, I find myself akin to Nan Shepherd, who also had a habit of wandering into the hills of Cairngorms without a purpose. 'As if meeting a friend,' Nan wrote about her walks to the hills. *As if meeting a friend*, I have come to echo her sentiment, thousands of miles away, in Hazaribagh.

Despite years of spending time with the waterfall at Salparni, I still slip on its rocks, returning with a sore arm or thigh, a twisted ankle or scratched skin. I joke that between the two of us, there exists a very physical, tempestuous relationship.

The stream at Salparni originates in Ichak.

After the forest gives it a shape, it becomes a river outside the woods. The river emerges at a village called Lotwa, where it makes a stunning natural waterfront. Here, it is called Deta. The Deta flows only for a few kilometres with its name. When it passes Lotwa, it meets another river, Kevta, in the reservoir of Lotwa Dam.

Built in 1975–76, a year before the forest was declared a sanctuary, the reservoir feels perfectly balanced to the eyes. It is a landscape of control, which, unlike Tilaiya Dam twenty kilometres ahead, satiates the senses but never overwhelms.

In summer, when the water shrinks, the red earth with its complex colonies of rocks is exposed to the feet. The sky domes over it with a light splattering of cirrus clouds. In the evening, the sharp sunlight turns the water ethereal. Dimensions deceive photography, and cameras fail to distinguish between the red, hard surface of the shore and the blue, fluid stillness of the water. This trick of light gives the place an extraordinary appearance. The reservoir, thus, floats on a thin carpet of air. In the sky, noisy egrets fly from one end of the water to the other. Through their presence, I discern my own. Lotwa Dam, hidden charmingly outside the forest, is one of my favourite places in the district.

'Every small town has this one old man, a prophetic grandfather, who knows everything about everything,' my senior and landscape photographer, Siddharth Pandey, made this observation in Delhi. Through the geographies of our towns, we have grown a friendship between the Himalayan mountains of Shimla and the Chhotanagpur plateau of Hazaribagh. I look at the pine trees in Shimla with wonder and Siddharth inquires about our mango trees in the plateau.

His statement resonated with me because I knew my town's grandfather.

He was my Bulu Uncle. It was at his place that I had first found Tiger Fall on an old, Coal India map. I had heard about it before and read about it in one of the old newspaper supplements.

According to the map, Tiger Fall was somewhere near the national park. I wondered if it was the waterfall at Salparni.

'Tiger Fall, huh?' I mumbled, studying the map.

'It is no longer there, Mihir,' Uncle replied from his desk.

He was occupied with his work on the computer.

'We knew it as Tiger Pool,' he didn't look at me when he spoke. I looked at the map, then at him.

'It is a stone mine now, can you believe it? I don't go there anymore.'

He paused for a moment, then, like a warning, said, 'It would be better if you also didn't.'

I was intrigued.

'But where is it?' I persisted.

Uncle lifted his eyes from the monitor.

'You know Lotwa Dam, don't you?'

Before Tiger Fall surfaced in the New Year supplements of local newspapers, it was documented by PC Roy Choudhury in the 1957 gazetteer of Hazaribagh. He described it as a place known as Tiger Pool, where 'the river tumbles over a number of small falls and rapids in a wild setting.'

Twenty-four years later, contributing a chapter to the book *Perspectives in Geomorphology*, authors Nageshwar Prasad and Md. Naseemuddin wrote about the presence of a waterfall in the same region. They also provided the coordinates in the article. Then, the authors mentioned Tiger Pool separately, quoting the same remarks by Roy Choudhury about the tumbling river.

It appeared that there were two waterfalls. The first was what Roy Choudhury and Bulu Uncle called Tiger Pool. The second was the one with the coordinates. I looked up the coordinates on the internet and stared in disbelief when the result took me to a landmark I knew very well: Lotwa Dam.

What happened?

Did the reservoir drown the second waterfall? It wasn't possible. Lotwa Dam was built at least six years before the book appeared in print. If there indeed was a waterfall at the coordinates, it would have disappeared into the reservoir long before the writing of the chapter. There was no way the authors saw the waterfall without noticing the reservoir. I reasoned that the coordinates were wrong. The waterfall which Prasad and Naseemuddin had mentioned might just be Roy Choudhury's Tiger Pool.

I have come to appreciate Google Earth.

In the absence of contemporary documentation, the software makes it easier for me to understand places. I knew from Bulu Uncle that Tiger Fall was a stone mine now, so I looked specifically for a mine near Lotwa Dam.

Sure enough, I found one a kilometre downstream from the reservoir. The satellite view made it clear that Roy Choudhury's river was Kevta, blocked twenty years later at Lotwa. I saw the impoverished river flowing into the mine. I looked at the terrain, tilting and rotating the view on the screen, but it appeared flat. No hills, no undulation. I was surprised, and confused. I had always thought of waterfalls as the children of hills.

My first visit to the mine was that summer.

Following Bulu Uncle's directions, I took the first right from the highway after crossing the national park forest. Two defunct gateposts welcomed me. Driving ahead, I crossed two more gateposts. An abandoned bungalow appeared in sight, its foundation covered with weeds and bushes. Dark, empty frames for windows and doors gawked in all directions. It looked like a forest department construction. A few weeks ago, at Ghaghra Waterfall located in Hazaribagh's Keredari block, I had seen a similar ruin. Tiger Fall, or whatever was left of it, had to be close.

I parked the Alto near the bungalow. The road before

me descended into the dry bed of the Kevta, emerging again on the opposite side. As I stepped out, I saw to my left a sheer fall of about a hundred feet, the sharp trough created by the mine. When I peeped into it, I saw bulldozers and dumpers at the bottom, hard at work. This was once the Tiger Fall. It was now dry, obsolete and ugly. I did not see Roy Choudhury's 'wild setting', nor did I see the tumbling rapids. The mine had hollowed the entire thing out.

I followed the river upstream. Before it could fall off the edge, the water was blocked deliberately by a small mound of earth. The bump stretched across the Kevta's width. Against the mound, a stagnant pool had formed. Further upstream, I found a small check dam. I stopped there, realizing that if I walked on, I would simply reach Lotwa Dam. I had seen what I had to see. After the first block at Lotwa Dam, the Kevta was systematically deprived of its water up to the edge of the cliff, the fall itself, so there was nothing left to spill into the mine below. I realized, uncomfortably, that the pleasing landscape of Lotwa Dam was created at the cost of Tiger Fall's disappearance into a stone quarry. A 2014 report published in *The Telegraph* had put the number of such mines at more than 1,500, stressing that the industry enjoyed the patronage 'of at least one minister and a well-known politician'.

I had thought of landscape as a stationary, geographical feature, defined by the physical appearance of things. In the distance between Lotwa Dam and Tiger Fall, it had turned flexible. It was a subject to economy, politics and public policy. No longer enduring, nor innocent.

That year, I waited for monsoon. When it arrived, it

also brought Vinayak, my school junior from Delhi. Like me, Vinayak too had studied English in the capital, and whenever he came to Hazaribagh, we would go to rivers and waterfalls. We had previously gone to find Ghaghra Waterfall together, and this time, we planned to find another one in the national park, near Pokharia.

Unfortunately, before the trip, I spent a sleepless night and it left me with little spirit to walk in the forest. We settled on going to Jihu, a village located on the outskirts of the forest. A different river flowed past it, and I suggested that we see that instead. We decided to leave the Alto and take Vinayak's motorcycle.

To reach Jihu, we needed to turn left after passing the national park, but I asked him if we could just check on Tiger Fall once and turned right instead. I was hoping that the Kevta's monsoonal flow would breach the mound.

We arrived at the abandoned bungalow and saw that the river had swollen substantially. It had managed to cleave a small channel through the mound from where the water escaped and dropped sheer into the mine. I was thrilled. For a better view, we walked around the edge, in a semi-circle, and were soon facing the fall. The visual of the mine leaped out at us. We saw the river falling into the pit, which was now a large pool. Due to excessive erosion, the water below was completely yellow. On the leftmost edge was another fall, created by the rainwater flowing through paddy fields and into the mine.

The mine had done two things to the fall: it had unwittingly increased its height, and had turned the place into a codependent system.

At Tiger Fall, the demarcation between natural and industrial landscapes was irrelevant. In summer, the dry natural encouraged the industrial. It offered the latter a platform. In monsoon, the wet industrial resurrected the natural, altering its size. What this synergy birthed was an invalid waterfall, devoid of hills, and with no forest for a shield. The bulldozers moved about the area below and Hyva trucks grunted their way in and out of the mine.

The wildlife census of 1991 recorded fourteen tigers in the national park. None of them survive today. Long ago, pugmarks of a lone tiger were found and the news had made it to the papers. What happened to the tiger after that is not known. Perhaps he went away, perhaps he was poisoned.

Earlier in April, 2017, I had taken my friend, Aditya, to the dry Salparni waterfall. We were classmates at DAV, and though we drifted apart on our own life paths, we have still managed to preserve our friendship from school. Aditya had come to Hazaribagh from the US on a short holiday, and I suggested we go to the forest for an outing.

'There won't be water in the fall, but it is still better than being in the town.'

My friend, debonair as ever in his shorts and t-shirt, and with a penchant for hiking, agreed.

Since the stream was dry, we opted to walk its course. At one place, we found a tortoise in the mud. At another, we ran into three axe-wielding men, locals from a neighbouring village. They were as surprised to see two urban dudes in the forest as we were to see them with their axes. After a quick hi-hello and brief conversation, we moved further upstream.

Later, as we returned, I told Aditya about Tiger Fall.

'It is somewhere close to the forest. Bulu Uncle says it's all gone now.'

'Like the tigers, *haan*, Mr Vatsa?' Aditya quipped. He is the only person who calls me Mr Vatsa.

I found his comment darkly amusing.

'But is there a possibility of return? Do you have any idea what it looked like? Were there hills around?' I asked Bulu Uncle one evening, many days later.

He recalled something and went to his office. When he returned, he came with a key. Then he opened an almirah and from one of the shelves, he pulled out a diary. With a red cover, it was the most distinctive of all the diaries stacked inside.

'Remember this red cover, Mihir.'

Uncle flipped through the pages. He seemed to be looking for something very specific.

'Here, take a look,' he passed it to me.

On the paper, there was a sketch. Actually, there were two sketches.

The first was of a picnic. A vintage car was parked in the foreground. The adults were shown carrying food from the vehicle in baskets. The kids had wandered off to the hills in the background. The hills weren't high, but they did make nice folds. Beyond the hills started a thick forest. A river emerged from it. It was the Kevta. It flowed down one of the crevices in the hills. The caption below the sketch said *Parking the car in the grassy patch above The Tiger Pool.*

The second sketch fully revealed the landscape. It showed a full moon sky under which the drop of the two hills formed the background. The Kevta came down from the right cliff to make a pool. A tiger approached the water. Then the river dropped one more time, making a second pool in the forest. In the foreground near the right corner, there was a rocky ledge which carried an inscription. The sketch was captioned *Tiger drinking at The Tiger Pool by a full moon*.

'When did you make these?' I asked Uncle.

'1952,' he said, always sharp with his memory.

I read the entry accompanying the sketches. The last line read, 'On one of the ledges, I had my name inscribed, "Bulu", and I was very proud of it.'

As a child, when I was building fragile little mud dams over monsoon streams on one side of Hazaribagh Lake, another boy on the opposite side was looking at fishes and water snakes passing through the aqueduct. When I was attending DAV School at the foothills of Canary Hill, he was studying at St Xavier's near PTC Chowk. When I went to Delhi to study literature, he went to Bhopal to study engineering. All the years that we were in Hazaribagh, with only a lake between us, we never met. Even when we were away from Hazaribagh, in our own separate cities, we never met. When we did meet, it was 2017. We spoke first on Facebook, and when we met later in person, it was by the lake.

Raza Kazmi is my soulman, a term I use endearingly for my best friends. I identify him with the forest of Palamu, he identifies me with the waterfalls of Hazaribagh. Together, we have travelled to many places in Jharkhand, running often after ruins, rivers and forests, making plans that surprisingly do materialize.

While Salparni lies on one side of NH 33, the larger forest of the national park extends on the other.

Its entrance is located at Pokharia, a kilometre before Lotwa Dam. From Pokharia, a laterite road traverses through a handful of forest zones. Pokharia forest comes first, followed by Jihu forest, Donai forest, Kaile forest, Horeya forest and Dumri forest. From Dumri forest, the road leaves the national park through another gate at Bahimar.

On this road, there is the small but scenic Baghmara check dam, the intriguing Tiger Trap built by the Rajas of Padma, and a ravine called Dhamdhama Maand. Earlier, the ravine used to be a tiger's home. Now, it belongs to some porcupine.

Sahil Ka Maand, or Sahil's Lair, the signboard enlightens visitors.

I think of my friend and former colleague Sahil when I read this phrase. I know that when he comes to Hazaribagh and sees this sign, he will be amused.

Sal trees command the landscape here too. At Horeya forest, the national park has its tourist centre. It is called Rajderva, the abode of kings. It is an old, royal hunting lodge which was upcycled to make the forest's principal rest house during SP Shahi's tenure in the plateau. Shahi also dammed a jungle stream here to create a lake. Its purpose was to provide enough drinking water to the animals while also adding to the scenic value of the place. Recently, a small but significant intervention by the forest department has resulted in the installation of a few perching logs in the water for the birds to rest.

A canteen with a dining hall was also constructed during Shahi's time, on a small island in the lake. The site, separated by a narrow moat from the road, could hold a small fortress. Shahi built watchtowers too. There are a few in Salparni and about ten around Rajderva. One forgotten watchtower, its staircase no longer there, stands deep inside Harhad forest. There used to be a forest rest house at Harhad too, but presently the structure looks similar to the abandoned bungalow near Tiger Fall.

One day, my elderly Facebook friend Zulfiqar Ali sent across a photo of the rest house. 'Early 1990s,' he said. 'We used to go to Harhad quite often. I have many fond memories of that place.'

Harhad is a village located on the Hazaribagh-Katkamsandi Road, a few kilometres from Bahimar Gate. The forest rest house was built on a small hill. Though the bungalow is in decay, on clear days, I can see it from the road. The view of sunset from its roof is unparalleled in Hazaribagh. Low-rising hills appear behind the sun. They hide many towns in their crevices. A short trek downhill is the Muhane river, rushing down the western escarpment of the plateau.

The crippled watchtower looks over the river crashing against the rocks.

In the autumn of 2017, we were a big team.

Initially, the plan was for Raza and myself to stay a night in the forest. It was something I had always wanted to do. Raza was a forest veteran. On WhatsApp, he would send me photos of the many forest rest houses where he stayed and where he wished to go. I, on the other hand, would get excited at the most trivial of constructions, reacting often with 'heart-eyes' and other precise emojis. When he floated the idea of staying at one of the cottages in Rajderva, the bait worked.

Raza knew Bulu Uncle too and wanted to meet him in Hazaribagh. We went together to Sanskriti, Uncle's home, and proposed that he come with us. He agreed to a day's trip. Elizabeth Aunty agreed too. We were also joined by my friend Shubhodeep, who was working at the time in Hazaribagh as an associate to the Deputy Commissioner.

As it often happens with big groups, we got delayed. Instead of leaving at one in the afternoon as Raza and I had planned, we took fancy to the lunch spread out on the table. By the time we had eaten, it was three already. We reached Ichak half an hour later and picked up Akbar *ji* from the Salparni rest house.

Raza and Akbar *ji* knew each other too. When Raza's father, Kazmi Uncle, was a Divisional Forest Officer in Hazaribagh, Akbar *ji* was one of his staff. Akbar *ji* had watched Raza grow up in front of his eyes, and true to the service culture, he regarded my friend with a mixture of love, respect and concern.

In Raza's Santro, the six of us adjusted. We entered the forest from Pokharia, and half an hour later, we were at Rajderva. It was five already. On our way, we crossed a sandy stream which Bulu Uncle remembered as Kekda Nala.

'There used to be so many crabs here,' he said. 'We would come here to find them trotting on the sand.'

As the evening pressed, there was no point getting Uncle and Aunty back to Hazaribagh now. We persuaded them to stay the night in the forest with us. Akbar *ji*, being familiar with the staff at Rajderva, went to the canteen to arrange for tea.

The first thing I remember from that night is the cold. The second is the bonfire. The third thing I remember are the ghosts.

We did not count the hours. It was a moonlit evening, and even when it got dark, I could see the crowns of the trees. The forest road was visible too, so was the black void of the lake. When silence descended upon the forest, we did not protest. When the lake made the surroundings chilly, we took it in our stride. At nightfall, we assembled outside our allotted cottage, started a small fire, and began with the stories.

We started with mundane conversation and anecdotes, aware that the night would most definitely steer towards the paranormal. There was also a lot of waiting involved. Raza and Akbar *ji* had driven out to get ration for dinner. During that time, Bulu Uncle, Elizabeth Aunty, Shubhodeep and I talked about many things to pass the time, but mostly it was Uncle talking about the past.

'I once saw X animal here. I once photographed Y animal there. In my time, photography was an art. Kids these days, they have no talent.'

Shubhodeep and I nodded and let out the appropriate *oh*s and *ah*s.

Later, in the dark, we tried shooting photos in the manual setting. Uncle assumed the role of our mentor. Shubhodeep succeeded. I immediately attributed his achievement to his fancier camera. I, on the other hand, gave up after ten blurred photos and put my Nikon back on landscape mode. We started the fire later on perhaps, when Raza returned. When he arrived, he saw us fiddling with our cameras in the dark.

I had hoped that he would put an end to the nonsense.

'What is all this, you are so dumb,' I thought he would say, but to my utter frustration, he joined in too. The charade of night photography continued for another half hour. Elizabeth Aunty looked as bored in her chair as I was in mine. Raza succeeded in getting photos too.

'Please, you guys have better lenses,' I complained. 'My camera is so basic.'

Eventually, we did release the ghosts.

After dinner, we took turns with our stories, unleashing *bhoots*, *pishaachs* and *chudails*. I recounted the rickshawallah story, Shubhodeep narrated one about the sly tigers in the Sundarbans. Raza told a chilling story about a young forest officer at Dudhwa Tiger Reserve and how he met a grizzly death under ominous circumstances. I won't even attempt to summarize that story here because Raza tells it far better than I. Besides, it is his story, not mine.

But the tales, once they began, went on without a break, as the night deepened into midnight. When we had released every ghost in the woods, we shivered, not knowing if it was the cold or the horror of it all.

Raza and I returned the next night to the forest.

The previous day we hadn't got much time to talk. Our conversations on WhatsApp and Messenger were internet-appropriate: light, banterish, laden with emojis. It was the forest which made us open up to each other.

In the rest house, we got the fire started in the fireplace. If you looked through a slit in one of the shuttered windows, you could see two men sitting adjacent to each other, their silhouettes glowing. We shared first our failures. How both of us dreamers often found ourselves lost and alone against the reality of our times. It felt right to talk about disappointments in this forest because, at some level, the forest was a failure too. In all the years that I have walked in the national park, I have longed to see wildlife. Even when I once walked the whole thirteen kilometres circuit from Rajderva and back, I saw only a tree felled by villagers and some cows.

I remember how, a few months later, Raza and I were joined by Rahul, our friend from Patna, who had driven to the park straight from Valmiki Tiger Reserve. Rahul had brought his camera traps with him, so after obtaining the required permissions from the forest department, we eagerly planted them in the forest. We felt very professional during the exercise, sure that this time we *would* find evidence of wildlife.

While testing the flash and the cameras' response, I played the deer. I was supposed to cross a skeletal river and the cameras would click after registering my shadow. I went, trotting and skipping down to the river bed.

'Hoo hoo hoo… I is deer… I is thirsty… I get water… gulp gulp gulp… now I meet frenz… hoo hoo hoo frenz.' The cameras clicked, the flash worked fine.

'Why does your deer do *hoo hoo hoo*?' Raza and Rahul were stunned.

Clearly they could not appreciate the finesse in my

performance. We decided to leave the cameras for the night and retrieve them in the morning. When the two of them brought the equipment back the next day, we saw only my deer's blurred photos.

There is a special quality in friendships forged by passion and a shared appreciation for the work of the other. With such friendships, we are able to create happiness in what appears to us as an isolated existence.

Raza is valued because as long as he was in Jharkhand with me, I didn't feel alone. I didn't feel like the only person running after forests, rivers and waterfalls, when the world was running after its own neat ambitions. Our ambitions were twisted. I saw in my future a teacher at a degree college in a small but picturesque town in Jharkhand. Raza saw in his future a wildlife historian or a forest officer who could visit as many old forest rest houses as he liked and spend nights there.

But we are very different too. He is hopelessly old and I am hopelessly young. He likes his forest rest houses preserved with their original red-oxide floors, while I would love to see a slick, Scandinavian-style forest rest house in the jungle. His nostalgia for the past finds a critic in my laboured optimism for the future. My extroverted Facebook profile is often mocked by his dormant account. But while at one time, we were separated by water, in the forest, the earth had brought us to friendship.

When the fire died at midnight, we couldn't stoke it back. Even the air inside the rest house's hall was disappointed.

'Wow, Raza,' I said, 'Such pros we are. Men of the forest, who don't know how to sustain a fire.'

A year later, Raza returned with a gift.

It was the first edition of FB Bradley-Birt's *Chota Nagpore: A Little Known Province of the Empire*. The book, published in 1903, is a lovely red hardback. The front cover carries a cobra in gold. With the gift, Raza proposed a drive to the forest. We were to go to the waterfall at Salparni and read there for an hour. When I messaged a friend in Delhi about it, he said it was the best plan that two men could make. Raza carried JW Best's *Tiger Days* with him. I had my *Chota Nagpore*.

It was an Instagram kind of day.

The month again was October. The sky was a clear blue, again. I parked the Alto before the bridge. It no longer had the pothole which was there seven years ago. With or without that pothole, it had now become a ritual for me to park the Alto before the bridge.

We had not seen enough rain during monsoon that year, so I was afraid the waterfall might be dry. But the sound of the stream hit me the moment I stepped out of the car. The flow was thin and weak, but there was just enough water for the fall to be personable.

At first, we tried finding nooks within the rocks, to be *right there* with the fall. It didn't work. The inclines of the waterfall might work well for pretentious photography (which I enjoy often), but to read properly we had to find someplace more comfortable, more level. We discarded the waterfall altogether and returned to the top, walking upstream.

Only a few boulders ahead, a perfect spot appeared.

Here, the stream flowed along against the hill, leaving

a nice, little beach by the side. I rolled out the mats on the sand. The sunlight was brilliant, the water was clear. Lying on my stomach and facing the water, I took the book out.

Something was still missing.

The sunglasses. *Of course, the sunglasses!* I put them on in slow motion, opened the book to chapter ten, and turned into an intellectual hero.

The tenth chapter in Bradley-Birt's book is titled 'The Garden of a Thousand Trees'. It is a direct reference to Hazaribagh. I have read the chapter so many times that I have memorized its first paragraph:

It is a picturesque title—The Garden of a Thousand Trees—and, if somewhat fanciful, yet given with a true touch of Oriental imagination and love for high-sounding words. A huge mango tope, containing a thousand trees, some of which still remain, was called Hazari, and round these a village grew, spreading in time into the modern town of Hazaribagh, the Garden of a Thousand Trees. Such is the interpretation of the name the oldest of the inhabitants give, one of them adding, with pardonable pride in his native town, that this is the Garden of Chota Nagpore, and that motto over the old gateway of the Emperors at Delhi might well be written of Hazaribagh:

'If there is a paradise on earth, it is here, it is here.'

North

Memories are not immune to ageing.

This is scientific: the brain filters out memories of events, places, people, feelings, keeping what it considers important and discarding what is not. The neatness in this is seductive.

Has it ever happened with you that you make a memory and forget about it, leaving it to go stale, so stale that you can no longer tell if it was based in fact or myth? I have some memories like that. They are fractured, appearing in faint spells, and when they show themselves, I cannot tell if the events transpired in reality or in my imagination, or whether their sources lay in my relations with the outside world or the people around me.

In one such memory, I am watching some hills covered in mist. In another, I am twelve or thirteen, looking out of the window of a vehicle, at the clouds gathering over the cliffs. *I wish I could ask the driver uncle to stop.* In the one following that, I have arrived at a cluster of hot water springs. It is Suraj Kund. Priests at the temples are haggling for money, and there is my grandmother. The next one is that of disappointment over not going to see a waterfall.

There are no more memories after that.

The north of the plateau is a broken, often disappointing, and surprising escarpment. It is seldom sheer, and therefore, not always impressive. It is less a dramatic elevation and more a series of bumpy, shoddy speed-breakers found on Indian roads.

To look for beauty in the north is to either renegotiate the concept or to subject the place to the existing codes of aesthetics. In some places, the rules of 'natural beauty' are well-defined, like in the mountains or with the oceans. An articulation of beauty exists for such geographies. There is so much literature about them, in books, images, videos, blogs, listicles. *Ten Things You Must Do in the Himalayas. Twenty Things to Do in Kerala. Do You Know About This Hidden Beach in Karnataka?*

Cliffs are beautiful, valleys are beautiful, waterfalls are beautiful, forests are beautiful, sunrise and sunset are beautiful, beaches are beautiful, sea shells are beautiful, the gulls are beautiful, and the boats moored in azure waters are beautiful. To be beautiful is to be perceived as such, it is to believe in the *narrative* of beauty, if not the phenomenon itself.

The plateau is beautiful as long as it shadows mountains in the escarpment. It is beautiful as long as the rivers are tumbling. It is beautiful in its forest. It is beautiful in its isolated hills. With few frameworks to understand the beauty of a plateau, I borrow. The charm of my hills is borrowed. The attraction of my waterfalls is borrowed. The silence of my forest is borrowed too. The mind finds in these tropes ways to hinge a landscape for examination.

To think that beauty could have rules, that land could

be made to yield—imagine our vanity in such desires! When I am in the north, I am at my most selfish. I hoard my expectations, knowing that they won't be met. I make unreasonable demands, knowing that they won't be fulfilled. I make disappointment a norm, and I codify this disappointment into an aesthetic.

Often the plateau disappoints, and in that alone lies its beauty.

I was at my friend Deepak's shop near Panch Mandir in the ludicrously crowded town. Deepak runs a travel agency in Hazaribagh, and I needed to collect a ticket from him. Because we have known each other for a few years, sharing also an appreciation for travel, we got to talking about Suraj Kund, the hot springs existing downplateau by the Grand Trunk Road in Barkattha. I told him about my first visit to the place.

'I was very young. Mother was there, and my grandmother was there too.' I was recounting the details that I remembered, and it was then that it arrived, that faint memory of people speaking, their voices a mild buzz in my brain, and I, a kid, listening.

'You know, they said there was a waterfall in the hills behind the Kund. It sounded very fantasy-like because they said…'

'I know what they said,' Deepak interjected, a sage expression on his face. 'They said if you went there, you would find colourful stones.'

I looked at him with astonishment, and disbelief. Astonishment, because there was indeed another person, sitting right in front of me, who had heard the same story.

Disbelief, because I never thought that the place could be real.

'*Aap gaye hain wahaan*? Can you tell me anything else about it?'

Deepak shook his head.

'Sorry, I have also only heard about it,' he said.

After I returned with the ticket, I began arranging my memories at home, asking Maate to fill the gaps where I couldn't. Now that the floodgates were open, what was before a barren patch was overflowing.

I remembered that the waterfall with colourful stones had briefly been an obsession of mine. I had included it in my famed list of 'places of tourist interest', which I made for my visiting relatives. These places were Rajrappa Temple (now in Ramgarh), Tooti Jharna (again Ramgarh), Itkhori Temple (Chatra), Canary Hill, Hazaribagh Lake, Suraj Kund, Barso Pani and others.

'What is Barso Pani?' someone would ask.

'It rains there when you clap.'

'*Aisa kya*?' they would gawk at me, bewildered.

'Well, that's what the papers say,' I'd quip. If the papers say so, it must be true.

In the living room, Maate and I pieced together whatever we remembered of our Suraj Kund trip. Neither of us could recall the waterfall's name.

'And why didn't we go there on the first visit?'

'There were reasons,' Maate explained. 'There was no road to it. They said it was a trek up the hill. We were also with your grandmother, remember?'

I remembered my grandmother on the trip.

'Forests used to be sensitive places then,' she said. 'We returned from Suraj Kund and went to Harihar Dham. That trip was more about seeing temples with your grandmother.'

For now, I am going to call this place X.

My attraction for X was short-lived. It faded a couple of years after our first visit to Suraj Kund. As life went on, not once did the thought of X return, not even when I returned home from Delhi and drove to the forest looking for streams and rivers. The north never appealed to me, and I had forgotten that X was in the north. *That area is so dull. That is not Hazaribagh.* X didn't cross my mind. Without a name, it was an undefined variable. I had forgotten X, I attached no value to it. It could be everything if I wanted it to be, and it could also be nothing.

A couple of years ago, the north held nothing for me except some hot springs by the Grand Trunk Road at Barkattha. There was a place called Chauparan, known for its sugary Kheermohan and a deadly stretch on the GT Road. This section of the road was often termed Khooni Ghati in Hazaribagh's newspapers. Then, there was a place called Chalkusha too. *Where the hell was that? Fake plateau! All fake plateau.*

My phrase 'fake plateau' is misleading. What I consider *real plateau* is the middle Chhotanagpur, the Hazaribagh plateau, and my perception of this highland is already a sum of borrowed aesthetics.

The flatland of the town is easier to understand because it resembles the plains. When the hot summer wind raises the dust up from the ground in a stunning swirl, Hazaribagh feels similar to Patna. The escarpment is easier to understand because it resembles the hills. When mist gathers over the range visible from GT Road, Hazaribagh feels similar to a North Indian hill town.

To travel north from the town is to approach Hazaribagh in reverse. Doing so *undoes* the plateau. It is to feel the temperature increase. Instead of going flat-up-flat—as one normally would to climb a plateau—we have to go flat-down-flat. Moreover, the Chhotanagpur exists in steps, and this makes it harder to submit the land to a singular aesthetic.

The 'fake plateau' is the lower Chhotanagpur, which, for the middle plateau, is a flatland. To go north from Hazaribagh is a downwards journey, but at the same time, it is also to go to the top of the lower Chhotanagpur. Lower, middle, up, down: so much happens in thirty-five kilometres.

My 'fake plateau', more than geography, is a notion unpleasant to comprehend. It is harder to appreciate because it evades the conventions of beauty that I have *curated* from other landscapes. The north is my nemesis. It bares my uncomfortable biases. It exposes my favouritism for the middle plateau, which is my home. The thing is, there is nothing fake about the *fake plateau*. It is so disarmingly original that it scares me to insecurity.

After Deepak had brought X back to the present, I took to Google Earth again.

I was now a few waterfalls old in Hazaribagh. They had begun to form a praxis through which I approached and rationalized the plateau. I understood water through them. I understood elevation and the escarpment through them. I understood human settlements through them. Google Earth made the charting of water easy. I saw streams turn into rivers, and I watched them flow through narrow valleys in the hills. When I tilted the view, the hills formed in 3D. Where I saw exposed rocks, I knew it was a place of interest. *Should check this out someday.* Where there were no rocks, I inferred it was either all water or the forest was too thick.

Often I confused forest trails with dry streams, and though I think I have now trained my eyes to differentiate the two in the plateau, the same eyes fail when I hover over the plains of Bihar.

There is a river that flows near Suraj Kund. Since it is the only water feature close to the springs, one evening, when I had nothing better to do, I opened Google Earth and started following it upstream.

Soon enough, the forest appeared and the elevation started. The folds in the hills appeared as dark lines. The river too started to shrink in width as I followed it up its course. First it made a ninety-degree turn and went inside the forested hills, and after following a straight path for about half a kilometre or so, it made a ninety-degree turn again. Here, there were many rocks. In fact, the whole path of the river was rocky. When I went further upstream, I saw that this river was formed after two minor rivers had met deep in the hills. The valleys of these two rivers were separated by a ridge. I was traversing the elevation to reach the tabletop now, and I followed each river up to their vague origins on the plateau. Both these rivers followed rocky paths, and after they met, the larger river cleaved a rocky path too.

How was I supposed to find my waterfall in this parade of rocks? There was not even one forest trail going into the hills. Which water body was I supposed to follow, which river in the forest had the more colourful stones?

A branch road from NH 33 goes to the temple-town of Ichak.

That Ichak is identified by its temples is confirmed by the myriad signboards announcing them all across town. Ichak is teeming with them, and like all places that exist with an abundance of temples, this little town too is languishing in its past glory. You could grow nostalgia here.

Ichak was once the capital of Ramgarh Raj, and traces of royalty are still visible in the town's old, ailing brickwork.

It was the kings who built the temples. When they shifted to Padma, they took the importance attached to these temples with them. In Ichak, the difference between divinity and its home becomes stark. It is one thing to believe in gods, quite another to believe in temples. I do not know if the people of Ichak are expressly religious. They seem to be, though I only know for sure that they have immense faith in their temples.

A few years ago, when I had gone to this town to photograph the ruins that exist today, I was greeted with many curious faces. After I had taken the photos and was about to return, a group of middle-aged men stopped me.

'Are you here for *sundarikaran* of these temples?'

I said I wasn't.

'We saw you with the camera and thought you were from the government.'

I confessed I liked the ruins and that I too was waiting for the promised *sundarikaran*, or beautification, to happen.

There exists a line between beautification and conservation. While one prefers the latter for historically and culturally significant sites, at places like Ichak, where nothing really happens, to expect nuance in these matters is to fish for intellectual luxury.

'*Sundarikaran*' is a stock word. When people with power run out of words to throw at expectant eyes, they resort to these cliches. *Sundarikaran*. The word is as hollow and made-up as it sounds. It means the exact opposite of beautification. When someone says *sundarikaran*, they basically admit that they have already given up on a place. *Sundarikaran* is a word that makes contractors rich and the *sundari*-fied place poor. It is a way to spend public money on places that are already *sundar*, already beautiful. It is such a hopelessly *sarkaari* word that it inspires no confidence in the people, and because it inspires no confidence in the people, it is a favourite with our politicians and bureaucrats.

But the road is lovely.

From Ichak, it goes to the hamlet of Kariyatpur, and from Kariyatpur, it goes to the village of Lundru. From Lundru, the forest comes into view again, and when it does, the plateau feels familiar to me. When the single-lane road reaches Karichattaan, the valley begins and the downplateau drive starts.

Sal trees sprout from the land to shoot up into the sky. When the sky is clear and the light good, the black tarmac shines. The open forest gathers depth as the elevation decreases, and the road adjusts to the contours of the escarpment. If the national park forest is a sly edge of the plateau, the forest in this part exposes the terrain, and also layers it. In the absence of vehicles, the visuals this road offers are stunning. Here, the hardly-sheer north points a finger at me and laughs. 'Take this, moron,' it says, and the moron takes it all in, greedily.

When the last stretch of the valley arrives, it brings with it sights of the flatland below. Here, on the left, I see the Mahabar hill range with pointed peaks. 'Egg Shell Mountain,' my friend Mirtunjay Sharma renamed it later on one of our drives.

'*Aaj se humlog isko yehi kahenge*, Mihir. There is one in China, isn't there? We will call this hill too by the same name.'

On the right, I see the escarpment reach its finale, meeting the flatland in the shape of an elephant's head. This hill is called Mahuda. When perspective plays tricks, I can go ahead and touch the animal's face. When reality cuts the illusion, I realize there is a river between the two of us.

My mother and I drove on this road for the first time in 2017 and became fans instantly. Long after we had left the escarpment and arrived at Suraj Kund, we were still drunk from everything we had seen on the way.

The road was truly breathtaking.

At Suraj Kund, we saw the five hot water springs again.

They are Ram Kund, Sita Kund, Lakshman Kund,

Brahma Kund and Suraj Kund. The last is the hottest, considered the hottest in Asia, and it unifies the five streams under its moniker.

But Suraj Kund is not pretty. It exists amid desolation. There is a word in Hindi to describe unbearable appearance of this kind: *ujaad*. Of course, at Suraj Kund too, *sundarikaran* has happened. Concrete is everywhere. Separate pools have been made for people to bathe in. An uninspiring rest house with locked doors has been constructed for no real purpose but to spend money. A hairpin road starting from one point on the GT Road, passing through the springs and ending at another, is operational. Suraj Kund is a *true* tourist spot now, with plenty of garbage adding leisurely to the attraction of the country's hottest geological wonder.

Behind Suraj Kund, mother and I saw the hills. We had come from there. The waterfall too was up there, somewhere, and so were the colourful stones.

Pundits crowded us again, asking us to see this temple and that, urging us to perform aarti for gods big and small.

'No one could make the roof of this temple, such is the power of god,' one of them started. For a moment, I seriously considered advising them to upgrade their scam. I was even going to throw in some Netflix shows, for good measure.

Maate and I had come prepared with tenners. There was no use haggling with the priests. Sometimes it is better to acquiesce and save the energy. Surely the god who didn't want a roof over their head wouldn't mind some rupees. We accepted the religion bubbling up in sulphuric springs, but before leaving the place, we asked a priest about the waterfall in the hills. He immediately shot back, it was too far off into the forest.

'Udhar toh koi nahi jaata hai,' he moaned.

I gave him a look. He gave us the name.

Nisanlagwa.

A year later, it was April.

The day was definitely cloudy, but with little chance of rain. Early in the morning, I started the Alto to see my colourful stones.

I was operating under three assumptions. First, that Nisanlagwa was a waterfall; second, that at the foot of the waterfall I would find the treasure; third, that it wouldn't rain that day.

The previous evening, I had opened Google Earth and surveyed the region again, the hills and the rivers. Because I had already driven down to Suraj Kund before, I had some idea of how high the hills of the escarpment would be.

I didn't think I would find a tall, plunging fall in those hills. The north still is the milder escarpment, so it wouldn't have waterfalls with a high drop. My fascination with Nisanlagwa was with the stones. It was anyway going to be a long river walk.

On the map, I discerned two approaches. I could either walk up the plateau from Suraj Kund, or I could walk down. If I took the former approach, the village to start from would be Chanudohar. If I took the latter route, my starting point would be Simradabh. I opted for the latter. It was always easier to walk downstream. Besides, if I did emerge at the top of a tall drop, I could just turn back and try again later from the opposite direction.

To reach Simradabh, I took the NH 100.

It is the road that goes east to Bagodar, where it meets the GT Road. I drove out of town, crossing the hills at Silwar, the BSF Camp at Meru, the lazy market at Jhumra, and the narrow Shakespearean arch bridge over Siwane river at Daru. The 1874 plaque commemorating the construction of the bridge is still embedded in the brickwork. Here, the river is most beautiful, flanked on either side by lush sal trees. Since it was April, the sal were also sprouting their tiny, light yellow flowers.

After crossing the bridge, I turned left towards Godhea. From Godhea, I passed through many villages to reach Narayanpur, from where the final stretch of road took me to Simradabh.

This stretch had been built recently, and the morning light pilfering through the sal trees cast an endless series of bar shadows on the smooth, black surface. When I reached Simradabh, I saw mud houses, their exteriors painted with the Sohrai colours of yellow and ochre.

Here, the Alto attracted the attention of the villagers.

The road ended in an open ground where I parked the car.

Stepping out with my bag slung over my back, I walked a few yards back to the spot where a mud road shot off towards the forest. Curiosity walked with me, mine and that of the villagers' in me. On the road, I couldn't look more out of place. I was like that novice anthropologist, who arrives at a village in immaculate kurta-pajama, thinking his *humble* attire would somehow help him blend in with the crowd. I wore a t-shirt and jeans instead, and though I saw women and children, there seemed to be very few men in the village.

'*Sab gel halthun baahre.* Everyone has gone out,' one of the women said.

A couple of times, I inquired with them about Nisanlagwa and saw their eyes widen. But they wouldn't say much. Some would just giggle. Unable to extract much information, I walked quietly to the village's primary school. A man wielding an axe, I saw, was coming along the mud road in my direction. I waited for him, hoping that maybe he would confirm the path. As he neared, I asked him about Nisanlagwa. I swear I saw his face betray a hint of bemusement. He asked me to repeat what I had just said, as if he wanted to really confirm that I did not mean anything else. Behind me, the women I had seen before had assembled. They whispered to each other in Khortha.

'*Nisanlagwa jaithun. Sachche, Nisanlagwa*! He wants to go to Nisanlagwa. Really, Nisanlagwa!'

I repeated the dreaded word again.

'Nisanlagwa is not here, you know, it's quite far,' he scoffed at me.

I told him I had all the time for it.

'See, I am here at seven,' I said. 'How far could it really be? Two hours, four hours? Why don't *you* take me there?'

The axeman laughed.

'I have work to do,' he snapped.

Behind me, the women continued to talk among each other. Two or three men had joined the crowd too.

My Khortha is elementary at best, so I only registered the word Nisanlagwa being thrown around from one woman to the other. The men only seemed concerned with staring me down.

Clearly, my approach wasn't working. With no viable option in sight, I did what any self-respecting man would do in my situation. I made a puppy-face and waited for it to melt the axeman's heart.

'I have come so far from Hazaribagh, will you turn me away?'

Neither my puppy face nor my emotional blackmail melted anything.

I still hadn't given up though. 'Fine,' I said. 'I'll go on my own. That way, right?' I pointed in the direction the axeman had come from.

He nodded. Behind me, the women continued chattering.

'*Nisanlagwa jaithun*. Nisanlagwa.'

I had caused an unceremonious village assembly on the road, and the more the attendees grew in number, the more flustered I got.

Leaving the crowd murmuring behind me, I started walking, taking the solitary mud road. How hard could it be? I had walked in many forests before. I could do it.

But then, the women did something crucial.

As I dramatically trudged down the road, I heard one of them ask the axeman to go with me. '*Jo na re, tohni ke kono kaajwa thode hi haw*. Go with him, no, you hardly have any work.'

I stopped, turned in his direction, and made the puppy-face again.

And so it happened that at seven in the morning, the axeman and I went off to see Nisanlagwa.

We took the mud road and walked straight into the forest.

The road stayed with us for some time, after which the plateau began to descend. The road too was replaced by a forest trail. On one side of the trail, I saw a group of petite mud houses nestled among the trees, and wondered how great it would be if I could simply live here. I asked my companion about the huts. They were his home.

'That whole cluster belongs to us,' he said.

There were some patches of land near the huts that had been cleared of the wilderness and turned into sowing grounds for paddy. In two months, the monsoon would arrive and fill these plots up.

I admired the view of the huts in the forest, their walls impeccably smooth with mud plastering. Mud houses in Jharkhand are always delightful to look at, and my new friend's little colony in the woods was a fine example of the architectural craft practiced in the villages.

After fifteen minutes of walking and covering roughly a kilometre, we arrived at a drop in the land. In front of me lay the flat slate of a dry waterfall. The river was almost non-existent. Only a streak of water trickled down tightly through the rock. There was too much labour in that motion. The river seemed like it was trying to save its last shred of reputation, before going into a sure existential crisis. Two more days of sun and even this trickle would come to a halt.

The clouds above were loose and without motivation. So far so good. I had consciously chosen April to see Nisanlagwa, because I wanted to gauge the accessibility of the place. Early summer was a good time. Without water, the river looked like a bad road.

'I told you before that you wouldn't find water here, but you wouldn't listen,' the axeman reminded me of my stupidity.

'Yes, yes, you were right,' I agreed. '*Aage chalein?*'

We went down the fall.

Small puddles of water formed in the sand, and in the nooks created by boulders. In the whole forest, there were only the two of us.

The river bed was not soft on the feet. Every step I took was marked by rocks and stones trying to offer my soles acupuncture therapy. Thinking of the walk as such made it bearable.

Curated Northern Experience
Experience Natural Therapy at Simradabh
Assorted Pointed Rocks Await

This was only the beginning, the starting point of the trek, my morning *nature walk*. I was excited to complete the full course, but I could have done with fewer rocks in the river.

Then, something unexpected happened. My axeman, who had so far been trying to dissuade me from following the river, started hopping from one boulder to the other, and motioned for me to keep up. I obeyed enthusiastically, and soon there were two men hopping on boulders in the forest.

I didn't know how far he would go, or when he would change his mind and just return, but going with him was actually better than going alone. I am not averse to solitary exploration, but I am also not silly.

This was definitely not the place to please an amateur's ego.

Once the walks, jumps and leaps on the river started, the valley began to clear up. Since we were also jumping from one available perch to the next, and not all stepping stones were on the same plane, we saw the hills rise and fall and rise again. We saw the land *form* from different altitudes.

The forest looked impenetrable, and the more we ventured into it, the quieter it became. It wasn't that the walk was particularly dangerous. What felt dangerous was the *isolation* of the place. Moving ten feet forward took much longer that it would on a tarmac road, and because the mind is conditioned to view distance in relation to time, it felt like we had been walking for an eternity. While actually we had only been on the river for half an hour.

We moved with the river, went wherever it took us, and turned with it. When we stopped, we found that we had arrived at the confluence of our river with the other one.

I had seen this exact spot on Google Earth. I had wondered about it then. Now I was standing here. Then suddenly, piercing the quiet of the forest, I heard a shrill cry. I looked at my friend, inquiringly.

'Peacock?'

'Peacock,' he confirmed.

'Anything else you see around here? Leopards, maybe?' I asked, hopefully.

'Not anymore.'

The two dry rivers met in a straight line, and where they met, they formed a sandy island. If they were carrying water, it would flow around the porous mound. Adhering to the typical millennial wanderlust rituals, I had recently bought a tent. On that island, I pictured pitching it in the sand and hanging a lantern on a staff.

High cliffs rose on either side of us, and on them grew sal trees resplendent with their new, light green leaves. Whenever the clouds separated in the sky, the sun hit us with the sharp morning light. We were in the plateau's depression—not above, not below, but *within* the escarpment.

The physicality of it was enormous and the phenomenon spellbinding.

My guide led the way again.

I do not remember the exact sequence of what happened next, but he found a spur on the cliff and I saw him leap up the steep incline in a flash. He was with me one moment and on top of the cliff the next. He glanced back at me and asked me to follow him up.

Throughout our walk, I was trying to impress him with my resolve to complete the route without a frown on my face, and throughout our walk, he engineered new challenges for me. We could have simply followed the river, which we had done so far, but this wasn't enough for the axeman. I suspected a few times that he was making the walk *a little bit* more intrepid on purpose, but I didn't want him to think that I was weak.

Two can play this game. Finding the spur, I put my left

foot on it and lifted my right arm to grab a sprouting branch. It was strong enough to bear my weight. Below the branch was another notch where I put my right foot, and hurling my body upward, I climbed. *Not my first time,* I showed him. At moments like this, I feel thankful that I've got a skinny, lean frame.

Once on the elevation, I saw my friend walk ahead into some bushes. *Really, bushes now?* I followed behind him, warding off annoying twigs with one hand and clearing the undergrowth with another. After crossing the bushes, we came to a faint forest trail that ran precariously along the edge of the cliff. One wrong foot, and a broken skull would be the least of my worries.

I saw my friend pass through the ledge easily. Now it was my turn. *Don't look down, don't look down. Just don't look down.* I did not look down, and passed too. When we reached a wider clearing ahead, I saw the river below make the second drop. This was waterfall number two. Though there was no water anywhere, it was easy to imagine how frightful the whole place would become in monsoon.

The river, after surviving the fall, crashes straight into a hill that rises abruptly in front of it. This hill would not permit the water to cleave through it, so it takes a sharp right, creating a jaw-dropping gorge in the valley.

'Which hill is this?' I asked.

The axeman had found a boulder for himself and was sitting comfortably on it. 'This is what you came for, isn't it? This is what we call Nisanlagwa.'

'*Yeh Nisanlagwa hai?* This hill? I thought Nisanlagwa was a waterfall!'

My friend said nothing, besides giving me a wide smile.

'*Achcha*, why is it called Nisanlagwa? Any idea?' I prodded.

He said he didn't know.

'Is it because there is a mark somewhere? A *nishaan*?'

He just shook his head.

The gorge in front of me was easily the wildest in the plateau.

It was so rough and so enchanting, I couldn't believe a place like this existed in Hazaribagh. For the longest time, Nisanlagwa was a myth to me. It was my X, a variable which could become anything I wanted it to be, and it was my ex too, in the sense that at one time in the past, I was infatuated by it. About this X, people had spoken without seeing it, and those who had seen it, were shy of sharing it. It wasn't the shyness which comes from protecting something valuable. Instead, it was the shyness that discerns in the other person their inability to reach the place. '*Bahut door hai*', 'You won't be able to go', '*Wahaan koi nahi jaata hai*'. How do you reconcile with a myth? Is myth a waterfall or is it a hill? Or is it the rocks? Is it dangerous or is it beautiful? Does it operate along neat binaries? I would call Nisanlagwa both dynamic and beautiful. Dangerous and rooted. I wouldn't call it ethereal. It had none of the lofty qualities that make a landscape transcend to something higher.

Instead, it was fiercely grounded to the earth. Huge rocks and boulders jutted out from everywhere, like scales on the body of a snake. Each rock was a different colour from the other, and though the colours were not vivid, it was not hard to see why and how Nisanlagwa got its reputation.

There were no stones that I could carry home with me. The few pebbles I picked up, I could have picked up from any river. The obvious attraction were the huge rocks.

I had come to Nisanlagwa looking for a waterfall and colourful stones, but I ended up according a much higher value to the rocks. Massive rocks that coated the river like a difficult, demanding sheet. The sand we had seen and walked on so far had disappeared in the gorge. There was no sign of it. There were no banks to the river either. The river was *crammed* between Nisanlagwa and the hill we had climbed earlier. It was clear that the water had fought cruelly with the land to earn its passage. When Nisanlagwa hadn't budged, the river demolished the hill next to it. From our perch, signs of that demolition were visible in the rocky fringes that erupted horizontally into the emptiness, their decapitated existence telling us that the violence was not over yet.

I returned from Nisanlagwa with a sense of accomplishment, and pride.

After all, I had looked at the clouds and correctly predicted it wouldn't rain that day, and also I had finally cracked a myth. I felt sure of my 'cloudcoding' now.

It was close to eleven in the morning when I got back home, and I recounted every detail of my walk to Maate.

'*Achcha*, tell me if I can also go there,' she asked.

'To the first waterfall, yes. There is enough of a road till there,' I said. 'Beyond the first fall, it will be tough for you.'

Maate's body is not immune to ageing. Just climbing the stairs to the apartment leaves her breathless. There is always pain in the joints.

The deal I have with her is that I do the initial recce, and if I am convinced that the place is suitable for her, I take her there. What she used to do for me earlier, I do for her now.

When she was a riverwalker, she too had looked for a waterfall deep in the forest. Dhara Fall, near Petarbar. It is the only waterfall in Jharkhand that she has seen and I have not.

Years ago, my relatives from Muzaffarpur had come to visit us in Hazaribagh. Our plan was to take them to Rajrappa Temple and return. I was forced to stay at home because of an exam the next day. When the happy tourists returned late in the night, they brought with them wild tales.

'The forest was so thick, the sunlight wouldn't even reach the ground.'

'We can't remember how much we walked.'

'There was a para-teacher who showed us the way. He was from the nearby village and you wouldn't believe how fast he walked through all that jungle.'

'Do you remember your Dhara Fall?' I asked Maate presently in the living room, transferring photos into the computer.

'Yes!' she exclaimed. 'To tell you honestly, I still don't know how we ended up there. We had only gone to see a temple.'

'Well,' I said, 'you could think of Nisanlagwa as my Dhara Fall.'

'Really, is it that dense, the forest?'

'It is frightening for sure and also extensive. If it wasn't for the axeman, I couldn't have done it on my own.'

We then talked about isolation, and how help arrives in unexpected places.

'My para-teacher, your axeman. Did you get his name?' she inquired.

'Yes, I did.'

I have chosen not to reveal his name here because I don't want people bugging him in the future.

'I also told him that I would return later, when there is water.'

The photos were transferred. I took the laptop back into my room. Outside, the clouds thundered.

The first drops seemed uncertain on the land, tentative, but soon it was pouring, angrily. It rained with so much force, I could hear vengeance in the water crashing against the earth.

I remember this rain well because when it came, I went out to the balcony, looked up at the dark sky, and felt my pride sting a bit.

South

There were three of us in the car.

We had reached a dangerous slope in the final leg of our journey. If we made it, we would save an hour, atleast. It may have been a forty-five degree descent to the village below. It may have been less, or more.

On any other day, I would have turned back. But that day, we were pressed for time, and I was operating out of an old vendetta against the road. It was a straight-forward escarpment path. You drove from the top and you arrived at the bottom. No bend, no turn, nothing.

Every metre the car moved, it did so grudgingly. My feet were glued to the pedals, my breath paused behind my pressed lips. There were so many boulders, so many rocks. The road was eroded. Deep gullies ran through it like veins.

'Creepy Road,' I had told my friend Sujit before we started from the town. 'We will take the Creepy Road today and hopefully we will survive.'

Ten thousand years ago, the prehistoric human lived in what is today the Karanpura valley. The impressive rock art at Isko village tells us this much.[15]

This valley, fed by forty-seven proverbial rivers and ending in the south of the plateau by the Damodar, is the most fertile region in the district. It is the rice bowl of Hazaribagh, giving the town its food. It is also one of the largest coal belts in the country, giving the nation its fuel.[16] It is home to the indigenous arts Sohrai and Khovar, now celebrated across the state as Jharkhand's pride.

This land is fertile also for archaeology.

A number of rock art sites lie scattered across the valley's length. One of the country's most sophisticated megalithic complexes stands here, at Pankri Barwadih village.[17] At least four rock-cut caves, belonging probably to the Buddhist period, are concentrated at one massive hill range, the Mahudi, alone.

Four major waterfalls, among plenty others, are found here: Amandhara-Bailgiri near Kurlungwa, Gittikocha downstream near Hahe, the monsoonal but sheer Dumaro at Mahudi Hill, and Ghaghra near Lajidag. A cluster of natural springs too is found here, deep inside the forest, near Bundu in Keredari. A gorgeous rock formation right on Hazaribagh's border with Chatra is here, near Tandwa. The mysterious Barso Pani cave is here, near Jhikjhor. There's an uncharted cave system at Isko. The ruins of an old fort are to be found here as well, at Badam.

A sprawling rose bush, planted over three hundred years ago by Raja Hemat Singh and his queen in front of Badam Fort, is found here, still blooming.

The Karanpura valley, comprising the administrative blocks of Barkagaon and Keredari, is a place ready for imagination, but it harbours a reality that is rife with conflict.

The valley suffers from abundance. Everything is in plenty here—the coal, the heritage, the scenery—but we have not yet devised a way to deal with this excess. Often the heritage comes in the way of coal, or the coal comes in the way of forest, and sometimes the forest comes in the way of humans. If not the forest, then the mining companies' grunting vehicles send unsuspecting travellers packing from the road.

A play of warning and consequence is staged in this valley, where lives are cheap and resources precious. Here, we are second-class, replaceable, subject to power games that are way above our pay scales.

Earlier, the valley was synonymous with terror.

The Naxalis in the forest were real, and the violence of insurgency in the region was a source for myth-making up in town. *Do not go to Barkagaon. Why would anyone go there? Don't you know about the dangers?*

To avoid dangers and enjoy only the brightness of a place is a luxury available to those who have a choice. For the people who live in the valley, the clouds remain. If previously, they were terrorized by the 'mamajis', today they are terrorized by the coal. If previously, they were an underdeveloped population, today their development is scripted under pollution.

I know Barkagaon as the place where I learned to love the landscape of Hazaribagh. In its flatness, I saw paddy swaying in the wind. In its ridges, I imagined waterfalls. In its forest, I heard stories of strange animals. *What exactly is a chhibba?* I learned driving on Barkagaon Road when it used to be a road and not a serial killer. Whenever I went to the valley, I knew I would return with new things, new sights—something which happens today as well. Though I am no longer sure if I appreciate the sights of the present: coal dust, hyva trucks, trees and leaves coated black like the tar on the road.

But this apprehension is personal. I have my priorities, the rest have theirs. Some places spark joy. Some places do not. Barkagaon does both, and it does so with flair.

On the very edge of the plateau is a village called Rajhar. Administratively, it comes under Katkamdag block, but below the village is the Karanpura valley, with Barkagaon's Badam as the nearest town. Sandwiched between the two man-made jurisdictions is the plateau's southern escarpment. Coming to this escarpment, therefore, is to travel from one administration to the other and back. This reminds me of my own territorial feelings about Hazaribagh and the neighbouring districts, about Jharkhand and the neighbouring states. I also recall how the hills, the rivers and the escarpments, simply by being continuous, natural forms dissolve the neatly-drawn bureaucratic boundaries.

At Rajhar, I had heard from Bulu Uncle about an emu farm, and discerned from Google Earth that there was also a waterfall in the escarpment. After my return to Hazaribagh in 2017, I needed a distraction to keep myself busy. When I found it, I found it in water.

A kind of madness had homed inside me that year, and this madness was to find waterfalls. They serve the same purpose for me as roads. I go to places through them. They are my tools to make sense of the plateau. Some people go looking for trees, some go looking for birds. I go looking for waterfalls.

Over the years, I have come to enjoy the rituals that are involved in following waterfalls. The road *will*, more often than not, end one to five kilometres before the site. The forest *will*, more often than not, begin after that. A river *will*, more often than not, require crossing. I *will*, more often than not, find a forest trail leading to the place. And I *will*, more often than not, find a guide.

Before 2017, the only waterfall I had known in Hazaribagh was the one at Salparni. Six years later, when I was home again, I itched for more. When I learned about Rajhar and saw it on the map, my hopes were raised. If there indeed was a waterfall close to the village, it would be my first after a long time.

We went to the village on a Sunday.

The car was packed. I was joined by Maate, my distant uncle Raj Chacha, his wife Anju Chachi, and their ten-year old son, Somu. While all of us were eager to see the emus, I was secretly rooting for the waterfall.

Rajhar was not really far, but because it was the first time we were going to that part of Hazaribagh, I made a list of all the villages we would cross on our way. If we stuck to the sequence, we wouldn't be lost. We were to cross Khapariawan, Marhand, Bes and Haram. After Haram, we would reach Rajhar.

To go to the waterfall, we needed to travel from Rajhar towards Motra and follow a trail into the woods. This road from Hazaribagh to Rajhar to Motra ended at Badam, a small town in the valley, where there are ruins of the old fort. This road was different from the main Barkagaon Road, with which we were familiar.

After crossing Khapariawan and at Marhand, we stopped a tractor trailing us to confirm if we were on the right path. If we were, then we should reach Bes shortly. The tractor driver was surprised to see an Alto on the road. This was understandable. The road itself was a narrow laterite strip of questionable merit.

Initially when we started, it looked fine, but when the road finally showed its colours, it didn't hold back. There were wide ditches and sharp bumps. Even the dull atmosphere made us feel unwanted.

'Yes… Bes.' The tractor driver confirmed. 'Is that where you have to go?'

Now, we weren't really going to Bes, but I also didn't want to tell him that we were headed to Rajhar. If he was surprised to see us at Marhand, I didn't want to alarm him further.

'I am going in that direction,' he said. 'You could follow me.'

We followed the tractor as it traversed through an unfamiliar landscape. Even though we were only a few kilometres away from town, this area of Hazaribagh was visibly different. Earlier, we had crossed a coal processing plant on our way and the land was black near the factory. Then we crossed a small pond with lotuses in it. The pond was the only pretty thing we saw on the road. We had met the tractor driver here, and as we moved through more villages with the tractor ahead of us, it seemed as if we had travelled back in time. Despite being close to the town, these villages looked primitive. They were sheltered by an eerie forest.

'This is not a good forest,' Maate remarked. 'There are more bushes here than trees.'

As we talked among ourselves in the car, the tractor in front of us stopped. The driver alighted from his vehicle and walked up to inform us that we had arrived.

'This is Bes,' he said. 'Where in Bes do you have to go?'

I was in a fix.

'Actually… we have to go to Haram,' I confessed, still not completely truthful.

If I were alone in the car, I am sure he would have looked at me with suspicion, but since we were a family, he was assured of our intentions.

'Oh, I thought you said Bes. Keep following then. I am also going in that direction,' he said.

We followed the tractor again. We crossed Bes station, we crossed the new railway line to Barkakana, and ten minutes later, we were at Haram. The tractor driver got down again, came up to tell us that we had arrived.

'Actually…we have to go to Rajhar,' I finally told him.

'Oof,' he made a noise. 'If you had to go to Rajhar, why didn't you say so before? *Chaliye, hum bhi udhar hi jaa rahe hain.* I am also going that way.'

We followed him again. The strangeness of the surroundings became more apparent after we had crossed the railway track. Barren patches lay next to a lush forest. There were not many houses. The air was still. From the moment we turned towards Marhand, the road had deteriorated with every passing village. It couldn't get any worse now. On the final stretch to Rajhar, we crossed a neat village called Kurlungwa, and after ten more minutes, the tractor stopped near a pond.

'Rajhar!' The man shouted from his seat.

'Emu... big bird... *bada pakchhi*... where?' I shouted back.

'*Udhar*!' he yelled, pointing at the road ahead.

After we stepped out of the car, I asked him if he had seen the birds himself.

'Only heard about them,' he admitted. Maate invited him to join us.

'*Isi bahane tum bhi dekh loge, beta*. You will also get to see them.'

As we started walking towards the enclosure, we noticed that the village was very quiet. No wind disturbed the leaves on the trees. Time too had frozen; we were invading its stillness. The huts were plastered neatly with mud, and I did not see any litter in the village. *Adarsh Gram Rajhar*, a signboard told us. We were impressed. There was a certain smugness to the village, a feeling that it was content with itself. When we reached the enclosure, the four birds inside looked at the six of us, befuddled.

Somu spoke in Maithili with Maate. '*Ki chhai? Imoo yaih hoi chhai*? Are these emus?' The birds made heavy bass noises. Maate humoured him. '*Jaanle, imoo lagg jaada nai jaihey, oo kaatai chhai. Hamar beta ki kaait leit ta humra budd dookh hait. Tu ta khoob budhiyaair chhe.*' She was telling him not to go near the birds as they might bite him. It would be painful for her to see her smart boy get bitten. On the side, I sniggered.

Seeing us at the enclosure, a couple of men emerged from the hut. They were the owners. Chachaji, the tractor driver and I spoke with them about the farm, how they made money from it, and what they fed to the birds.

'They give us one thousand for an egg,' one of the men told us.

Somu, after getting bored with the emus, took a liking to a baby goat and picked it up in his arms. When it was time to leave, I took photos: Somu carrying the goat, Maate and Chachi with the birds, and a selfie with an emu.

When I confessed to the tractor driver that I wanted to go to the waterfall, he was shocked. Genuinely stunned.

'There *is* a waterfall here, isn't it?' I prodded him.

He said that there was, but he had not seen it.

'*Bataiye*, what kind of a local *aadmi* you are,' I teased him. 'You hadn't seen the birds, and you haven't seen the waterfall either. *Aapko humlog hi ghuma dete hain.*'

'*Ab* what can I say, *bhai*? I take this road only because of work. You tell me, who stops here and there like a lunatic on a desolate road?' He was right.

'*Khair*, I know the way,' I said, and pulled out my phone.

It took an era at Rajhar for the map to open. When it loaded, I showed him the route. 'It starts a little ahead from here, on the way to...what is it called...Motra, yes, Motra. See, I am carrying my camera too.'

As I spoke, his expression of shock morphed into that of concern. I knew this expression. I had seen it appear on the faces of people whom I met in the forest every now and then.

'If what you are saying about the route is correct, then I suggest you take your photos quickly and not stay there for long. There are still...,' his voice lowered at the last word.

'Mamaji?' I offered. He looked around, as if making sure that we weren't being watched, then nodded. I looked at the people who were with me. We were two men, two women and a child. It was still morning. *Morning should be OK.*

'Where are you going now—Motra?' I asked him.

He said he was.

We followed the tractor again. If the road we had taken to Rajhar was bad, what followed afterwards was worse. The terrain rolled sharply.

It first went down down down, and then it went up up up. We were caving inside the escarpment. The uncomfortable forest also started with us. There was something not-right about it. Maybe it was the remoteness of the place, or maybe it was the absence of any sound. There were no birds in the sky either. There was only the laterite road which was broken, and ahead of us, the tractor. *We shouldn't be here.* It didn't feel safe.

An element of foreboding began to work inside me. This was a very creepy road. It made me conscious of myself. When we reached the spot where I thought I would find the trail, I saw that instead of a path, it was a dead stream. A dry rivulet. The approach to the stream was blocked by a pile of rubble, three feet high. I looked at Maate. I may have been able to climb over it, but she certainly couldn't.

'Better go back,' she advised.

We were still pondering our next move when from the opposite direction emerged two men carrying coal on their bicycles. This was illegal coal, sourced from mines that were closed for extraction. Made brave by poverty, these men risked their lives every morning to chip off whatever coal that remained inside the shut mines. If, by any chance, the roof collapsed and they were trapped, it would be their misfortune. They crammed the coal into white, plastic sacks on their cycles. The first sack was inserted into the triangle between the two wheels, while two more were fastened on either side of the carrier's ribs. Securing the cargo this way, they lugged their bicycles up the escarpment and finally to Hazaribagh for sale.

The miners, when they saw us in the forest, looked shocked too.

I think, that day, we were all shocking each other. We stopped the miners and asked them if they knew the way to the waterfall. 'This path is *toh* gone,' one of them said, pointing at the stream and the rubble. 'You will need to go to Kurlungwa now, and from there you will need to turn right. *Uske baad*, go straight till you reach the last house. One Mundaji lives there. He will show you the way.'

Maate and I thanked them for the information. We then turned to the tractor driver and thanked him for escorting us up to this point.

'We should head back to Kurlungwa,' I said.

'Remember what I told you before,' he said. 'Do not linger in the forest. This is not that kind of place.'

I told him we wouldn't.

When we arrived at what we thought was the last hut at Kurlungwa, we saw two men working in the field.

If Rajhar felt sparse, Kurlungwa was sparser. There were fewer houses in the village. The quiet was pervasive. This time, I asked Chachaji to do the talking. He stepped out of the car and went to speak with them. The men too were curious after seeing us. I saw Chachaji explaining to them the place which we wanted to see. When he returned, he returned with company. The man's name was Shukkar Oraon. He was old, short, and tanned.

'I will take you,' he said. 'It's not far.'

We followed him on foot into the forest, and after walking for hardly five minutes, he brought us to the water. It was a small, stupid pond. Maate and I looked at each other, amused. Clearly, there had been a misunderstanding. Since I don't speak Khortha that well and since Chachaji had failed in his only mission, I turned to Maate for help.

'*Eee naai dekhtun. Paniya geero ho... kenne*?' she tried, miming the gesture of water falling from a height.

It took her a few attempts, but Shukkar Oraon understood her.

'*Paniya taarpo ho! Enne kenne, u ta khubbe door*! It is very far,' he said.

The word *taarpo*, we realized was the key.

Maate asked him if he could take us there. Shukkar Oraon mumbled, looked at us, then agreed. When we returned to the car, the packed Alto was crammed even more. Chachaji went to the back, Somu went in his lap and Shukkar Oraon joined me in the front.

We would have easily lost our way if it wasn't for Shukkar Oraon.

I had only driven for a few minutes when the road, like a tree, disappeared into a network of branches. In every direction a path shot off. Shukkar Oraon kept me on track with his precise instructions.

'This way,' he would say, pointing left. 'That way,' he would say, pointing right. After crisscrossing the stray paths, we reached what was indeed the last hut of the village. Here the road ended, and in front of us was a river. We found our Mundaji too, drunk nicely on rice beer, splayed under a tree.

Crossing the river was easy, even for Maate. There wasn't much water in it, and like most plateau rivers, there were plenty of rocks for sure footing. Despite less water, the river had retained its flow. Once we were all on the opposite side, Shukkar Oraon led us into the forest.

It was January, the very first month of my homecoming. Frail leaves had begun to drop from the trees, obscuring the trail under a crunchy, yellow-green carpet. As we went further into the forest, I realized we were climbing up a hill-in-the-making. The river below had sunk deeper into its valley.

Chachaji and Somu walked behind Shukkar Oraon. Chachi followed them fourth in line. Behind Chachi, Maate and I walked. Since Maate was wearing a sari, it was difficult for her to navigate certain stretches of the trek. Often we lost sight of the people ahead of us and I had to shout in the forest, asking them to slow down. At one place, there was a huge tree trunk that blocked Maate's way, and by the time I got her past it, the team ahead was already out of sight. At another place, the slope was so steep and the gravel so loose, it made the descent dangerously slippery for Maate.

Then one time, I lost my patience with Chachaji who wouldn't stop even after I asked him to.

'Don't forget that this is *my* waterfall. *I* have brought you here.' I told him sternly, surprised at my tone and also at my use of the possessive pronoun. 'If *I* am not rushing, how can you?'

The adventurers slowed down after that. Sometimes the river below would disappear and in its place would rise another hill. Then one turn later, the river appeared again, even deeper inside the valley. We walked for about half an hour in the forest. Maate maintains she walked longer.

'You can say half an hour if you want. I know I walked at least for an hour, maybe even more,' she told me later.

We kept on the trail, following Shukkar Oraon, and hoped that we would soon reach the waterfall, that it wouldn't be another pond, and that there wouldn't be any mamaji waiting for us.

It was not a pond.

We had reached the top of the waterfall, which was a sharp plunge. Before the drop, the river pooled in the forest, depositing sand at one corner. From there, and through a narrow slit, the water rushed down a sequence of minuscule bends and steps before falling sheer into the larger pool below. In Jharkhand, the water pools that are formed after the river has made the drop are called *daah*.

At first, I saw only the *daah*, and I had to push my neck out over the cliff to find the image to the sound of water falling. It was the only sound in the forest. In fact, even we were talking to each other in hushed tones.

If a waterfall forms in steps, like the one in Salparni, it does not matter if you arrive at the top or the bottom. You can climb down the rocks to enjoy the full view. If a waterfall forms as a plunge, it is more practical to approach it from below, upstream the river. Initially, I thought I wouldn't be able to go to the *daah* because the drop was so sharp. Shukkar Oraon also said that going down was not possible. I looked at the surrounding terrain, searching for a spur or a ledge, and figured that if I descended from the left, there might—*just might*—be some support to make it happen.

How I managed to reach the *daah*, I don't know. It must have been the enthusiasm, it must have been the madness. I must have negotiated a few outcrops, some nooks in the rocks, or taken help of the branches that came my way. But I did reach the bottom of the fall. The view was finally complete. There was a thin band of water falling into the *daah*. A larger, sandy beach formed next to it on which I stood. All around me, hills rose, engulfing the waterfall in a loose embrace, and with it, engulfing us too.

It was a little past noon, and since the winter sun in Hazaribagh brings excellent light, the landscape was vivid. When Shukkar Oraon saw me get to the *daah*, he climbed down the fall as well. I had slung a tripod with me throughout the trek, so after I was on the sand, I released it and fixed the camera on it. The first photo I took was of the waterfall. The second photo was a self-portrait, a sophisticated selfie. The third was a photo of me and Shukkar Oraon together.

In the last one, I made a silly, horizontal V sign at him, happiness visible on my face, while he stood next to me like a rock, staring blankly at the tripod.

That same year but months later in summer, my friend Sujit came to Hazaribagh. I had first met Sujit in Delhi, and our friendship had developed through wine, cheese and poetry. In that particular order.

The first day, I took him to the watchtower at the edge of Canary Hill forest, and from there, we went to Siwane river near the arch bridge at Daru. The next day in the afternoon, I suggested we take a road trip.

'We may discover a waterfall, but we will definitely see some emus.'

The waterfall I had in mind this time was different. It was made by the same river that flowed past Kurlungwa, but it was located a few kilometres downstream from the one I had visited with the family. This new waterfall was accessible through road.

'We *would* need to walk a bit into the forest, but it wouldn't be a long trek,' I said.

There were two routes to it.

The first one was a longer road. I could drive from Charhi through Jorakath village to reach Badam, and from

Badam, I could drive north through Ambajit village to reach Hahe. At Hahe, the river's final fall marked the end of the southern escarpment and the beginning of the Karanpura valley. This route would take two hours to complete, one way. The other was much shorter. If things went smoothly, we would be there in an hour.

But there was one problem with this route. It was the same old creepy road between Rajhar and Motra.

'We will take the Creepy Road today,' I told Sujit. 'It's dreadful as hell, but hopefully, we will survive.'

We were also joined by Vinayak, who was in Hazaribagh at the time. I took the same road that I had taken in January to reach Rajhar. We crossed Marhand, we crossed Bes, we crossed the railway track, and then we got lost.

Instead of turning towards Haram, I took the road straight to another village. The first few minutes, I thought I was driving in the right direction, but soon it became clear that I had messed up. A passerby too confirmed this.

'You should have turned left after crossing the railway track.'

I should have turned left after crossing the railway track.

After a quick U-Turn, we reached the tri-junction again and drove towards Haram. This was the correct way. We crossed Haram, we crossed the church at Kurlungwa, and we crossed the river before Rajhar. I hadn't noticed the river from the road on the previous trip. It was the same river that flows past Kurlungwa, makes the plunge fall in the forest, and arrives at Hahe.

I took a peek from the window to check if there was any water in it. Not much, only in patches. Like the river, we too would be going down the escarpment. For a brief moment, I thought about turning back. There was almost no water in the river, so the chances of finding the waterfall dry at Hahe were high.

But then, I reasoned that perhaps it was better if the waterfall was dry. Besides, I wanted to go beyond the point where we had met the miners in January.

I wanted to complete the drive on Creepy Road.

A road could be dangerous for many reasons.

It may be prone to robbery, it may have been made shoddily. There may be potholes, there may be sharp turns.

Creepy Road was dangerous because it seemed to have been made for everything else but driving. I had looked it up on the internet once—*Motra Ghati*—and what my search returned was not encouraging. A couple were robbed, then another couple were robbed, then a few more people were robbed. There was a report about how people from the nearby village, frustrated at the apathy of the administration, took it upon themselves to fix the road into motorable shape. There was another report about a group of citizens handing a petition to the administration to get the road repaired. Someone blamed the delay on someone else. The files weren't moving. The regular drab bureaucratic drivel.

One time at home, I was speaking with one of my mother's colleagues about the places one may visit in the district. When she heard me say Motra Ghati, she couldn't believe it.

'*That* is a really *kharaab* road,' she said. 'Even though I have friends living in the villages nearby, I could never gather the courage to take that road.' Aunty had a Bolero jeep. I had the Alto.

Fortunately or unfortunately, we were a courageous lot in the Alto.

After crossing Rajhar, the road entered into the forest and the hills appeared. I approached it with the kind of humour we approach an imminent horror movie reveal. *I know you, Creepy Road. I see what you are doing. Oh, the familiar silent hills trying to scare me already? Oh, now the deep menacing forest. So we are going down down down now, eh? And now we will go up up up. Classic Motra [Chuckles].* If I knew a tune to play my thoughts on, I would have gladly hummed to keep the fear at bay.

After we crossed the dead old stream (the rubble was still there), I started anticipating what would come next.

Do not linger in this forest. I remembered the words of the tractor driver. We rose up and down with the road one more time and took a couple of turns. So far so good.

'It's not *that* bad,' Sujit remarked. I was feeling slightly disappointed.

'I can do these roads,' I agreed. 'I thought it would be way worse—'

No sooner had I finished my sentence that we went up an incline again. When we reached the top, what I saw was terrifying.

Fuck.

What did I see?

Not a road. Certainly not a road. It was a harsh, bare and rough escarpment. The only thing that made it look like a road was the laterite. Whoever had made the alignment the first time was clearly not paid enough. This was the last stretch. If we crossed it, we would reach Motra. We saw the huts a hundred feet or so below us.

On what was supposed to be a road, I saw a faultless demonstration of high school geography. There were trenches, there were little hills, there were valleys, there were boulders. If it rained, a river could very well originate from this man-made planet.

Not a soul was in sight—ahead of us, or behind us. I gauged the terrain, measuring with my eyes the width and depth of the trenches and gullies.

'*Chala jaayega*? Will it go?' I asked Sujit.

It was going to be tough. More than for me, it was going to be tough for the poor Alto.

Except for when the wheels hovered free in the mud, and except a few loud thuds suffered by the car's bonnet, we managed to drive down to Motra. Throughout the descent, the imminent wreck of the car flashed before my eyes. Throughout the descent, Sujit did the navigating—*cut here, slow down slow down, gently up this rock now, cover the ditch, down this rock*. It was truly a battle of nerves, and though I am prone to parading my emotions everywhere, I was surprised at my restraint. When we reached the huts at Motra, I saw a woman look up in our direction and then at the Alto.

'*Ee roadwa kakhano bantawo, chachi*? This road has no future!' I shouted at her.[18] She laughed off my complaint.

We did eventually find the waterfall at Hahe. It was dry.

We found it after walking for some time into the forest, not too deep. Unlike its sister fall upstream, this waterfall was far more accessible, forming in pleasing steps. We didn't choreograph our positions, but Vinayak, the youngest among us, climbed up the fall. I, older than him but younger than Sujit, climbed halfway, and Sujit stayed at the bottom. Later, Sujit christened it a 'resting waterfall'.

It was true. In the plateau, waterfalls do need rest. The summer is for their nap.

I returned to Hahe that same year, later in the monsoon.

The waterfall, I saw this time, had come thundering back to life. I heard it the moment I stepped out of the car. The river was bright yellow, with all the soil it had eroded from the plateau above.

This time, a boy from the village ended up accompanying me. I met him by the road, close to the spot where I had parked the car. I asked him if he would come with me and he agreed. But there was also an air of nonchalance about him. My attempts at friendly queries were reciprocated with disinterested looks, nods and shrugs.

Before reaching the waterfall, we had to cross the flooded river. I looked at the current uncertainly. For that boy, however, it was child's play. He jumped lightly from one visible rock to the other, and waited for me to follow. Not wanting to bruise my fragile ego, I took the risk and went in. Gravity pulled harder at my legs in the water. Walking against the flow became laboured. Still, I pushed on. The boy stood ahead, perched over a rock in the middle of the river, looking back every now and then at the clumsy *bhaiyya* following behind.

Usually I rely on branches for support during such times, so I instinctively lifted my hand towards a nearby shoot. But at that very moment, my foot slipped over a rock and the poor branch came apart in no time. I fell crashing into the turmoil below, the current sweeping me back by a good few metres. I went under the water, and in that brief moment, terror gripped my body. *Stupid, stupid moron. Dude doesn't know how to swim but will go looking for waterfalls in monsoon.* Half-floating, half-skidding and half-drowning, I caught hold of another branch hanging over me. This one held my weight and I was soon able to readjust.

Nothing happened. Nothing, absolutely nothing happened. No one saw.

When we arrived at the waterfall, I noticed there was no discernible *daah*—everything was inundated. The bushes were completely submerged and the trees had their trunks sprouting up from the rushing water.

'What do you call this waterfall?' I asked the boy, panting.

'Gittikocha,' he answered, not particularly to me.

Gitti translates to stone chips in English.

'That's a strange name. Why do you call it that?'

'I don't know,' he said, 'there used to be gitti on the top.'

'And what is this river called? Do you have a name for it too?'

'Dumuharwa,' he replied.

'And why is that?'

'Because,' he turned towards me in a playful manner, 'it looks like a snake with two heads.'

I was floored.

It didn't make sense then, but it does now. Adjacent to Gittikocha is another, minor waterfall, made by a different stream. I saw it a year later in 2018, with another group of friends. The two rivers meet at Hahe, and at the confluence, it looks like a snake with two heads.

'Do you see many animals here?' I asked him on our way back to the car.

Soon we would be out of the forest.

'Years ago, there was a leopard,' he said.

'Now, one last question. If I came to your village again and wanted to see you, what should I tell people? What is your name?'

'Md. Danish Ansari,' he told me his name.

'So, Muhammad Danish Ansari...'

'No! Em Dee Danish Ansari,' he corrected me. Then he smiled, 'But you can call me Tiger. Everyone calls me Tiger here.'

I used to wonder, if at the time of our drive down to Motra in the Alto, the creepiness of Creepy Road was real only for me or if Sujit and Vinayak too felt it.

Two years later in 2019, I messaged Sujit about it.

'I'm afraid not,' he replied. I was disappointed. It felt like an assault.

It couldn't be. To make sense of this, I started rationalizing. I had never really driven outside Jharkhand. Maybe what I called creepy in Hazaribagh was not actually creepy. Maybe it was the road's infamy that made me think so. Maybe it was the tractor driver's warning that winter, two years ago. Or maybe it was just the deathly silence of the place. When I asked Vinayak the same question, he said it was creepy enough. Then I remembered what Maate had said earlier about her trek into the forest with Shukkar Oraon:

'You can say half an hour if you wish. I know I walked at least for an hour, maybe more.'

The day after Sujit's message, I took my friend Mirtunjay Sharma to Rajhar.

'Let's go see some emus,' I texted him. Every time, the poor birds would be my alibi.

We went on his bike, and I resolved not to say anything about the road to Rajhar, or the Creepy Road afterwards to Motra. I wanted to know what he thought of the place.

When we reached Marhand, Sharmaji made his first observation. 'This is not a good place. I do not like it.'

'Uh hmm,' I shrugged.

When we reached Bes, he made his second observation. 'Really, do you see this land? It is so *beehad*, desolate.'

'Uh hmm,' I shook my head, noncommittal.

We spotted a palash tree blooming far away. It was flaming, lush with the bright red flowers.

After we crossed Haram, Sharmaji made his third observation. 'Baba, where have you brought me?'

I laughed.

We arrived at the pond near Rajhar, where I had parked the car two years ago. Here, we saw a bulldozer at work on the road towards Motra.

'Motra Ghati *bana rahe hain*? You repairing the road?' I shouted at the driver from the bike. He gave me a sullen look. It was the quintessential face of boredom mixed with annoyance, which the people in Jharkhand have for each other. '*Lerh* look,' as I call it. The person sitting beside him was more friendly.

'Will the bike go to Motra?' I asked the congenial one.

'*Haan haan*, it will definitely go,' he replied.

'*Theek hai*, okay,' I wobbled from inside my helmet.

We left the bulldozer to its work and went ahead to the emu enclosure.

The four emus gawked at us. I also made faces at them, miming a conversation. '*Onek dushto hoi jaabe*. So naughty you have become.'

I don't know why I switched to broken Bengali with the emus. A man emerged from the hut across the road. I didn't recognize him from my previous visits.

'Are these yours?' Mirtunjay Sharma asked him.

The man nodded. He looked friendly too. I told him about the time I had come to Rajhar with my family.

'We also went to the waterfall in the forest,' I recounted.

'Haan, boys from the village go there for picnic,' he said.

'We went from Kurlungwa. Shukkar Oraon showed us the place.'

As I talked with the man, we heard a sudden yelp from behind. It was Sharmaji admonishing a calf.

'He kicks!' he exclaimed, and then joined us outside the hut, smarting.

I only wanted to *show* to Sharmaji the descent down my Creepy Road, that final stretch to Motra.

After we saw it, I told him we would return. I was confident that since we were on a bike, it wouldn't be tough to reach the spot. We started on the road and went through the first undulation. Down down down, we went. I saw that the high rubble that had previously blocked the dry stream had been removed. Then we went up up up, again. As we reached the lip of that ascent, the valley below came into view. We stopped here to take photos.

Ahead of us, the road went through a pass, bordered on

both sides by a high landmass. It felt new, as if the bulldozer had only recently sliced the hill.

'Look, Nathu La!' I pointed at the pass.

'Ha, as if!' Sharmaji sneered.

We rode through the pass and when the view opened up again, I saw we had arrived at the descent to Motra. Here, another bulldozer blocked our way. Behind us, a bike appeared. There were two men and a girl sitting on it. I wanted to test my intrepid companion, and see if he would go down the road. There were no rocks or boulders this time, but there was at least a foot-high mass of dust blanketing the road. I stayed mum, waiting.

Mirtunjay Sharma started on the descent. The bike behind followed after us.

We passed the bulldozer through a narrow gap by the side. The only challenge now was to manoeuvre the bike through the dust sponge. I glanced behind to see how the other bike was faring, if its rider too looked anxious. But before I could see the expression on his face, I felt my axis tilt. The sky skewed and the trees lifted up. Both Sharmaji and I had crashed theatrically on the ground. We landed sideways on the soft dust cushion. The bike grunted beneath us. Mud was all over my arms, and my black trousers were now yellow.

'*Thhooo thhoo*,' I spat mud out of my mouth.

Mirtunjay Sharma too was covered in dust.

'*Tum na baba*, you are cursed! The other day at Chauparan with you, my car conked off and we had to return in a damn Hyva. *Tum poora humko jal-thal-vaayu* tourism *karayega*. Now you are working your evil tricks on my motorcycle!'

'Oh, come on!' I laughed. 'Now you are a bona fide veteran of this road! All thanks to me.'

Behind us, the bike with three passengers stopped to see if we were okay. They too were laughing.

'You saw nothing,' I told them, feigning seriousness. 'Nothing happened, you understand? When someone asks you if you saw anything funny on the road, you will say *no*.' They grinned widely.

'Baba, let's go back,' Sharmaji said, dusting the mud off his clothes.

'*Ab kya*!' I protested in good humour. 'Now *toh* we are almost there. I am going to just walk now. You come with the bike. We will return through Jorakath.'

When we reached Motra, we stopped by a tree under which a Pala period statue was sheltered. I went to take a look, wondering if I could identify the deity. I could not. When I returned, I saw Mirtunjay Sharma already in conversation with the villagers. We asked them if they knew when the statue had been unearthed. They did not.

'It was here before we were born,' they said.

'Do you know which god it is?' Mirtunjay Sharma asked me. I shook my head.

As we prepared to leave, one of the villagers looked at Sharmaji's dust-soiled bag and asked in a dulcet, mischievous tone, '*Gir gaye thhe kaheen kya*? Did you fall?'

I started laughing. Sharmaji started laughing too. So much for keeping it a secret. 'Yes, but you are not to tell everyone about it, okay?' I told the villagers who, seeing the two of us chuckle, started laughing too.

Territorial Trespassing

I want to say some things about rivers.

Eight kilometres west of Hazaribagh is a small reservoir called Chharwa Dam. It was constructed by the DVC to supply water to the town. Unlike dams that are built on discernible rivers *on* land, Chharwa Dam's purpose was to harness an underground water system supported by the monsoon and the flow of the Muhane river nearby.

A depression in the land along the north-south axis occurs at this site. Here, a slim stream would appear in the monsoon, disappearing again into the ground with the departure of the rains. After a part of this depression was deepened and the barrier put in place, the reservoir began to show.

Besides supporting the town round the year, the water also supports migratory birds in the winter.

Keen birdwatchers from the town flock to the reservoir with their long cameras. Opposite the dam, old rocks that once lay in the path of the thin river still stand. This miniature valley cultivates its water underneath the ground, and when the plateau begins its northward slope, the water makes its landfall—*landspring*—near the village of Pabra.

Here our first river, the Siwane emerges.

The Siwane skirts along the low Pabra Hill, changing its direction from north to the east. At Bonga, it passes under the NH 33, the road to Hazaribagh from Koderma, one that I've taken countless times when riding the train back home. Now that Hazaribagh town is expanding, it appears that the Siwane at Bonga will soon define its northern boundary. The river, eastward still but leaning south, flows behind the eastern towns of Meru and Daru.

At Daru, it draws an arc in a sal forest and turns completely south. Betraying its initial direction, the Siwane meets the NH 100, the road from Hazaribagh to Bagodar. It was here that a Shakespearean arch bridge was built in 1874, for the convenience of Sir George Campbell, the then-Lieutenant-Governor of Bengal. Campbell was fond of Hazaribagh. It was a town he admired, in some respects, even more than Darjeeling. I have walked on and with the Siwane below this bridge, alone and with friends. The river is stunning between November and March, its flow disjointed by rocks. Gurgling streams of water crash and flow into each other.

Not too far from this bridge is a village called Murki.

Now let us shift our sights about ten kilometres south-west of Hazaribagh town, to Banadag village. A railway siding was recently constructed here to load the coal from operational mines on to the trains. The NH 100, which in these parts of the district is called Lepo Road, runs through Banadag. Across the road is a reservoir called Gonda Dam, and behind Banadag is the forest extending all the way down to Barkagaon. From Gonda Dam, a trickle of water starts due east along the outskirts of Hazaribagh town, its chief utility being that of a *shamshan ghat* (cremation ground) *nala* at Khirgaon. Across the road at Khirgaon is also the Muslim cemetery.

Back at Banadag, a handful of streams also meet inside the forest. It is the origin of the Konar, our second river. The Konar begins flowing eastward and cuts the Barkagaon Road outside the town near Khapariawan. From Khapariawan, it flows past the Naman Vidya School and meets the *shamshan ghat nala* at Masipirhi. The Konar goes under NH 33, the road from Hazaribagh to Ranchi—through Koderma—and flows through the forest behind the Agro-Tourism Centre at Demotand. After travelling as a narrow channel in the woods, it widens at a village called Lara. A long, natural riverfront forms here and the Konar is dramatic in this stretch. It tumbles down spans of rocks in small steps surrounded by a sal forest.

Today, this riverfront has grown popular with Hazaribagh's residents. Boys and girls pose with their bikes, sunglasses, and other accessories. In the New Year, picnickers crowd the river, leaving styrofoam utensils everywhere. The waste lives from winter through summer, as the river also shrinks. When monsoon arrives, the pollutants are washed down with the Konar's overflow. It is a neat system.

When the plateau makes its eastward slope, the Konar enters the forest again. At Kewalu, it meets the quieter Jhumra-Churchu Road. A temple for Goddess Chandi is located here, close to the river. In this temple too, like the one at Suraj Kund, the roof could not be built. In some places around Hazaribagh, it seems that divine beings dislike a roof over their heads. This, according to the priests, is always an '*adbhut*' mystery. From Kewalu, the river courses towards the Daru-Churchu Road at Magarpatta. Here, the Konar is wide and sandy, the deposits showing a decrease of almost 300 metres in altitude. When the river reaches Murki, the Siwane is waiting for it.

At the confluence, Siwane is wider of the two, but it is Konar that gets to keep its name. Siwane, despite its delightful quirks and friendly rocks, despite also being my favourite, disappears into the Konar amid idyllic and heartbreaking surroundings.

When the Konar, carrying also the water of the Siwane, leaves Murki, it reaches a bridge. This is the bridge of Beram, which, unlike the arch bridge over Siwane, is a recent construction. Below the bridge, the Konar is pristine. Whenever I come to this bridge, I see in the water a shadow of the Siwane. I gauge the dissolved river's presence and feel betrayed for it. The Konar contributes, ushering its calmness through patches of sand, but the Siwane's rocky presence exists at Beram too. The water collecting into pools and puddles reminds me of my walks along the Siwane near the arch bridge at Daru.

The Konar bridge at Beram, however, is also an unfortunate structure, blasted off on one side. Whatever remains of it leans into the water below. Whoever detonated the bridge did so partially, leaving a small path open, yet hanging. Tractors creep through the hanging road. My Alto too creeps through the hanging road.

When I ask people nearby about the bridge, some of them smile. They don't remember the year it was crippled.

'Don't the officers at the block office say anything about it? Doesn't the MLA?' I ask them. I realize I am always aggravated. They move their faces from side to side, as if they no longer care, and walk away.

The road to Beram passes through Murki, where an interesting hillock stands outside the village. Sal trees rise from this mound. A tidy alley, wide enough to accommodate the Alto, runs through the mousy hill. The path's impeccable integrity restrains me from driving on it. When I come to this place, I come harbouring awe. I park the car on the tarmac and walk up to the mound. A loose magic floats in the air. When I look closely at the laterite track, I notice stones placed neatly in straight lines along either side of the path. I notice they are fixed to give the path its borders. A rushing traveller will miss it. A disinterested driver will miss it too.

This stone-bordered path is a human intervention to landscape. With no construction tenders and without resorting to concrete, the path is a work of the villagers' labour. No boisterous signboard takes credit for the '*sundarikaran*' here. No corporation passes it off as their CSR activity. The villagers merely declared their love for the land.

'I love you,' the lover says, and offers gifts. The lover sings. The lover dances. The lover writes of his love on the sky. The villagers used the stones from the land to gift the place a new charm. They did not give up on it, they used no words to codify their affection.

When I drive on the NH 100 and cross the turn to Murki, my head turns towards the river, the bridge, the hillock. 'Oi, what you looking at?' someone asks, and I say nothing, unsure if my sentiments warrant articulation, unsure if any articulation will resonate.

Big dams in the plateau have a sea-like quality to them. Summer is their low tide and monsoon brings the high tide. When a river is blocked to create a reservoir, it continues to be fed by the water running into it. This merging of the river's incoming flow into the reservoir's still water turns the place into a faux-estuary. Swathes of land are exposed when the water recedes in summer, exhibiting shallow canyons and valleys. The same canyons are submerged when it rains, the reservoir brimming with the monsoon's surplus, the water yellow with the eroded soil brought in by the flooded river.

When the Konar, having swallowed the Siwane, leaves Murki, it leaves the village to form its own sea at Banaso. The dam is named after it: Konar Dam. While the reservoir is scenic at times, it usually sports a dull appearance. The water, unlike Tilaiya Dam's reservoir on Koderma Road, is not always clear and blue. It often looks muddy, and when the sediments settle, it acquires a cloudy, turquoise colour like the water at Chharwa.

Like seas, large reservoirs too can confound the eyes.

In the years that I spent travelling across the plateau, I would occasionally work with the district administration on some of their projects.

The first among these assignments was a coffee-table

book on Hazaribagh Tourism, which my friend Shubhodeep and I had made together. After Shubhodeep completed his tenure at the collectorate and left, I became Hazaribagh's 'coffee-table book *wale bhaiyya*'. I made two more books for the administration, one on the Swachh Bharat Mission and the other on the 2019 Lok Sabha elections, both of which were received well in the administrative circuit.

I enjoyed working with tight time-frames, not unlike the brief but familiar grind of advertising, and the opportunity to observe the workings of the bureaucracy, which so far had been a mystery to me. Besides, I had an official *sarkaari* vehicle arriving each morning to pick me up.

This caused much surprise among the residents of our apartment building, who, aware that I was otherwise a night owl and probably a mystery too, would find me dashing off to the Sumo at seven in the morning, camera and tripod slung across my shoulders. Secretly, I would smirk.

I had the license to travel. I couldn't have asked for more.

One day, I had gone to a village called Barhamoriya while working on a coffee-table book. The village is located at the edge of the Konar Dam reservoir's buffer.

As the Sumo took the village road, I saw the water at a distance, shimmering on a plane which was higher than my horizon. I couldn't make any sense of this at first, but I soon realized that the altitude of the reservoir was slightly higher than the altitude of the village. If the reservoir was the sea, then Barhamoriya was below sea level. It was a jarring sight at first, later an amusing epiphany, and something I had not encountered before at any reservoir in the district.

Often, Konar Dam appears to be existing in a vacuum. The haze is strong towards the west. And because the dam is not anchored by hills, driving here too can be monotonous. However, when the monsoon leaves and the sky is clear, a high mountain appears in the west and transforms the view.

This mountain is the south-east edge of Hazaribagh plateau and also its highest point. With an altitude of roughly 900 metres, this is the plateau's end, or the beginning. The British recorded it as Jilinga. They turned it into a picnic spot for themselves. For the longest time, the only way to reach the top of the mountain was through horse riding.

Today, this massif is called Jhumra Pahad. It falls in the district of Bokaro, not Hazaribagh. It should not to be confused with the much smaller Jhumra Pahad near Jhumra in Hazaribagh. The Konar, after leaving the reservoir, flows along the eastern side of this high mountain, still in Hazaribagh. Rushing southwards towards Gomia, a town located twenty kilometres ahead of Konar Dam, it tumbles and drops at several places as the plateau descends. Before arriving at Gomia and near the village of Narki, the river widens to a surprising extent and falls through separate, swift channels into the valley below. This is Konar Waterfall, known locally as Chandru Jharna. It is the widest waterfall in Hazaribagh district. It carries water throughout the year.

South of Jhumra Pahad, and coming from the west, is one more river yet obscured from the view. This river will shortly meet the Konar at Gomia.

Raza Kazmi, thanks to some rare miracle, was on time that day.

'If you are going to portray me as a *late-lateef* in your book, then remember this hour, this particular moment,' he declared with a victorious expression on his face. 'Today, I have washed the stain off for good.'

I picked him up at Charhi, early in the morning, and we set out to drive to the top of Jhumra Pahad. The mountain, until quite recently, was notorious as one of the bastions of the Naxalis. After driving for half an hour, we reached the foothills of the mountain and realized that we were no longer in Hazaribagh district. The village by the road was called Rehwan. We had crossed over from Hazaribagh to Bokaro district.

I had imagined that driving up Jhumra Pahad would be an experience similar to driving on the twisted ghat roads of Netarhat, Jharkhand's highest and arguably the most scenic plateau, located 250 kilometres from Hazaribagh. But when the road started, it took us through sharp inclines with only a few bends. With each turn on the road, the Charhi valley below appeared larger. The houses shrunk into the bowl, and the already expansive landscape spread out even more.

Since we had planned to return the same way, I did not stop at many places to admire the scenery. 'We will take photos later,' I said. Halfway up the mountain, we reached a village called Jamnijara. Here, I saw something that reminded me of Himalayan towns. There were houses built by and below the road, cropping up in shallow depressions abutting the path. I had seen such houses in Uttarakhand and Himachal Pradesh. Now it feels like a proper mountain, I thought.

The next village we crossed was called Radium. 'I kid you not, it said Radium!' I exclaimed in the car. 'Maybe it was Raadium, or Rediyem,' Raza offered. 'We'll check the spelling later,' I said. Everything was shelved for later. Radium was a cluster of mud huts perched along the shoulder of a hill. In front of the huts, I saw Swachh Bharat Mission toilets. After my SBM coffee-table book stint, my eyes would often inevitably look for toilets in villages. '*Yahaan kaam hua hai*. They have done work here,' I would observe, passing through one village. '*Yahaan kaam nahi hua*,' I would remark, passing through another.

At Radium, the new concrete toilets blocks, painted white, were impossible to ignore. I couldn't decide whether to be annoyed by the white eyesores or be impressed by the reach of the Bokaro team.

When we reached Jhumra, we were disappointed. The village could have been beautiful; instead, it was littered heavily with garbage. Modernity had arrived here with concrete houses and RCC roads. Plastic was everywhere. There were shops with music blasting from stereo systems and large speakers. Nothing more than a nuisance, these speakers are called 'DJ' in Jharkhand. Seeing these DJs, I wondered what the world-famous DJ Khaled or DJ Snake would make of their local, machinic counterparts.

Before driving up to the mountain, I had scanned the internet for news about the region and found a nice article written by a policeman. In it, he had mentioned that there were little streams and waterfalls at Jhumra Pahad which were worthy of a visit. There was also a note about how the mountain was 'safe' for visitors again, easing my worries about the '*mamajis*'. Hoping to see the sights, we started chatting with a few people at the village. They were not particularly helpful. They scrunched up their faces and denied the presence of any streams, waterfalls, viewpoints. '*Neeche* Konar Dam *hai*. We go there only,' one of the men said. 'Really, there's nothing?' I asked again. '*Idhar toh waisa kuch nahi hai*...nothing,' the man replied.

It was improbable for a mountain this extensive to not have streams. Either the villagers didn't want us to venture into the forest or they were too preoccupied with work to show us around. 'If I drive straight from here, will I reach Konar Dam?' I asked. 'Yes,' they said. 'They are making the road, but the car will go.'

I remembered we hadn't taken photos while driving up the mountain, so we went back to Radium one more time. The village was indeed called Radium, the signboard confirmed. Unlike Jhumra, a laterite road went up to the huts there. We didn't go to the village, though we lingered by the sign for a while, looking out at the huts from the road.

At Jamnijara, the valley appeared into view again and we stopped at intervals. On one stretch, I drove and Raza took photos. On another, he drove and I took photos.

'Not like Netarhat,' Raza remarked.

'No,' I admitted. 'But it does have similar potential, no? We could plant some pine here; it is the right altitude.'

Raza suggested that we should think of our drive not as one to Jhumra but to Radium.

'You're right,' I concurred. 'Radium has the *feels*.'

I didn't want to take the same route home. The villagers had already said that the Alto could go down to Konar

Dam from Jhumra. Besides, we had driven from the west, so it was only apt that we finished in the east. We drove up to Jhumra again, not stopping in the village this time, and came to the road that would take us to the dam below. From Konar Dam, it was easy to get back home: Banaso to Bishnugarh, Bishnugarh to Hazaribagh.

When we started from Jhumra, the road felt different. The forest surrounding us was denser, and there were no villages dotting our way. The road also made sharp descents. I was beginning to enjoy the drive. At some places, the forest opened up to show the valley sprawling below. From some places, we saw flashes of the reservoir too, its water fading into the horizon. High hills with thick vegetation rose around us. 'There must be bears here,' Raza remarked, pointing at one of the hills. 'And this is a much better approach to the mountain,' I added.

'You know, it's in these parts that the police do their combing operations. They did it quite recently too. It was in the papers,' I told Raza. We agreed that on our next visit, we would take this stretch of road to Radium. 'It will make a nice circuit,' I had already started planning. 'You drive to Konar Dam, go up the mountain, and return via Charhi. A day well spent. We can advertise it, you know, like honest ads. Let's see… how about "Naxaliyon ki Rani, Jhumra Pahad"… sorry, "Jhumra Pahadi"? Too much? Do you think the Naxalis would mind? I don't think they would mind. Maybe the police would.'

Besides the Konar, the forest behind Banadag, close to Hazaribagh town, yields another, third river.

It originates near Fataha on the Barkagaon Road, and though it does not show itself in the town, it flows prominently through another city. In fact, it gives that city its name. This river, as long as it remains in Hazaribagh, is an escarpment river. The hills and forest never quite leave it.

Starting from Fataha, it flows under the Hazaribagh-Barkakana railway track to reach Bes. At Bes, it meets the Hazaribagh-Rajhar Road, the precursor to my Creepy Road. From there, the road turns south-west towards Rajhar, while the river turns south-east and flows sneakily along the outskirts of Hupad. From Hupad on the plateau to Sarbaha in the valley below, the river is a complex entity. As it comes down the escarpment, it collects between the hills to make clear, immaculate pools. Elsewhere, it flows by the sand which it deposits on the way. Often it rushes down the rocks, and often it flows over rocky sheets.

Before it reaches Sarbaha, the river births a legend.[19]

Once upon a time, a domesticated bullock strayed inside the forest. After several days of patience, he had finally managed to escape the village shed, venturing into the woods outside. By the river he grazed, and when the sun flared, the animal took shelter amid the lean sal trees. He remained there for many hours, waiting for the sun to wane. When dusk approached, he rose and drank water from the river. He didn't want to return just yet. 'Maybe I can stay here a bit longer, or forever,' he thought. 'I will live on things which the forest gives to me.' As he assembled these thoughts, his reverie was interrupted by a noise above. It was a couple of parakeets talking to each other. The bullock didn't mean to eavesdrop on their conversation, but he also couldn't help listening.

There was a tiger in the forest. He had killed a deer a couple of nights before, not far from the river. The birds said he might be lurking for more. This tiger had a reputation. For long months, he would disappear from the jungle, leaving the animals lax. When they were convinced that the tiger was gone, he would suddenly reappear and ambush his prey.

When the bullock heard about the tiger, he decided to leave the jungle right away. 'I will follow the water,' he reasoned, 'That way, I will find my way back to the village.'

He walked with the river, in the direction away from the forest. After some time, he reached a place where the river fell from a high, convex sheet of rock. Terrified, he froze at the sight. It was too much. There was no way he could make it down without slipping. But he looked at the descent again. 'Maybe,' he thought, 'just maybe, if I placed my hooves cautiously, I might just get down.'

Going back into the forest was not an option.

He took a step into the fall, but what he didn't know was that at this waterfall, he was not alone.

The tiger, of course, had already seen him. He had seen him by the river, and watched him walking away from the forest. He had stalked him all this while and now he was waiting, crouched behind the bushes.

At the waterfall, the bullock was too engrossed in finding a way down to sense any movement. Like an apparition, the tiger emerged from the vegetation. With soft paws, he crept up to the poor bovine, silently. The bullock, oblivious to an outline growing behind him, put another hoof forward, and the tiger sprang at him.

The bullock felt a huge weight crash against its body and immediately lost his balance. Both animals tumbled down the rock with a loud roll, into a narrow gulch below. Here and there, the outcrops struck them both in the head and limbs. At the landing below, the bullock was trapped. His hind legs broken. There was no place for him to run, he just could not get up.

The next morning, the farmer came looking for his bullock with some villagers. He saw the blood on the rocks, slivers of it still flailing in the water. The unfortunate bovine was nowhere to be seen.

When the men surveyed the area, they found a mark on one of the rocks. It was the mark of a hoof. '*Barad pichharwa*,' the farmer told the villagers, pointing at the mark. 'It slipped here.'

Decades and centuries later, one of these hills in the forest was sliced to make way for a railway track. The forest was largely spared. Today, this legendary waterfall is called Baratpichharwa. It is located thirty kilometres from Hazaribagh, close to Sarbaha village near Charhi. At Sarbaha, a milestone refers to it as a *picnic sthal*, in letters scribbled by a villager. In the forest, a river falls down a convex sheet of rock, announcing the end of the escarpment.

This, our third river, originating in Hazaribagh district, is the Bokaro.

The Bokaro, after its life in the forest, runs into coal in

the valley of Charhi. It also leaves the district of Hazaribagh and enters Ramgarh. It flows below the plateau and passes the mining towns of Tapin, Parej, Burughutu and Ghato.

A difference in colour occurs here, on either side of the Charhi-Ghato Road. On the north, the land is reddish-brown or yellow, adhering to the Chhotanagpur's pantone. On the south, it is black, covered in coal. The trees too look different here. Near the mines, they are mostly ghosts, their leaves hardly discernible to the eyes. Across the road and opposite the mines, the green of the leaves remain.

The fact of the lower altitude registers soon with an increase in temperature. Sweat forms easily on the skin. If the car windows are down, coal dust settles on it. Humans find their bodies sticky, black veins appearing on their limbs. When Hyva trucks grunt their way in and out of the mines, they release dark clouds behind them, eclipsing the light and the road.

In a country where the colour black is reserved for the disgraced, the people driving, living and working along the road suffer this humiliation daily. The land endures perpetual violence, watching the wounds on its surface fester and widen with every truck that enters the mines. It retaliates by throwing up coal all over the bodies of the perpetrators.

People die slowly here, and in pain. Coal invades their lungs, settles on their faces, defiles the walls of their homes. Even in winter, the sun is strong, the heat irritating. Some abandoned mines are reclaimed by nature. Wild grass grows on the high rubble hills that form in precise, unearthly geometry. The pits hoard rainwater, encircled by the black waste. Those who can, get clean water. Those who cannot, live on these ponds. The Bokaro exists as an aberration near the mines. It takes too much prime real estate, and is also toxic.

When the river emerges from the mines, it is much wider at Danea, where it enters Bokaro district. A railway station lends an air of importance to the place.

Danea could have been beautiful too. It *must* have been beautiful, at one time. At least that's what Bulu Uncle told me. Here also, like Jhumra, plastic waste was everywhere. Danea is located at the foot of the plateau, below Jhumra Pahad. The escarpment rises over it. Across the river, Lugu Hill with its precipitous cliffs becomes visible.

Lugu Buru, as the hill is locally known, is a sacred site for the Santhals, its sanctity protected by a thick forest cover that makes the range glorious and terrifying. This hill is home to its eponymous goddess Lugu Buru. There are several folk tales speaking of the hill's purity and how the goddess doesn't spare trespassers. In these tales, people straying into Lugu Hill's forest are often teleported to a cave and kept there for days or years. When they reappear in civilization, they do so with no recollection of their abduction or the time that has gone by. Lugu Buru in the past may have been a part of the plateau. Indeed, it looks like a plateau: it has a flat top and roughly the same elevation as Jhumra Pahad across the river.

If today the hill is separate, carrying a legacy of its own, it could be because of the Bokaro. This does make a good story: imagine the river cleaving a landmass, breaking it into two mountains across from each other. The river, it appears, has given Lugu Buru its own identity. At Danea, the Bokaro widens, then trims. When it leaves the village, it enters a straight, shaded gorge, flanked on one side by the high Jhumra Pahad and on the other by the majestic Lugu Buru.

In monsoon, both these landmasses are covered with mist. Unable to discern their heights, their beginnings or ends, the eyes are forced to admit a most delicate view, a view also hopelessly nebulous, into our finite, rational minds.

For three days, Vinayak and I canvassed this part of the river.

On the first day, we drove to Danea, but finding no feasible path down to the river and upset by the coal on our limbs, we returned home. On the second day, we approached it from the opposite side, from Gomia. We drove past Konar Dam, past Narki and Konar Waterfall in the forest, and past also Gomia's gunpowder factory. We saw that Gomia was bordered by the Konar in the north and the Bokaro in the south. We drove through the town, cursing the traffic, looking at the old houses and observing the shops. 'District Bokaro,' noted many signboards on the way. We had entered Gomia after crossing the bridge over Konar and we left it after crossing the bridge over Bokaro. We saw the Bokaro wide and sandy, well on its way to meet Konar near Bokaro Thermal Station.

We arrived at Tenughat after driving through Gomia, and here we saw another, *fourth* river making its way into the region. This was the larger Damodar. The Damodar, after its controlled release from Tenughat Dam, meets the combined waters of the Bokaro and the Konar a little ahead of Bokaro Thermal.

Here, the three rivers of the Hazaribagh plateau—the Siwane, the Konar, the Bokaro—end their run. The Damodar takes over.

We didn't go to Tenughat Dam, which is built over Damodar river. Instead, we took the Lalpania Road along Lugu Buru. From this road, we could see the two highlands, Jhumra Pahad and Lugu Hill, drop into the Bokaro river's valley. I had figured out earlier that if we were to approach the river from Gomia, we would need to start our walk from a village called Pindra.

Pindra was located at the foothills of Lugu Buru. It was here that the river was most solitary. Like Danea on the west, it was the last village on the east. There was only forest after that. And the river. When we reached the turn to Pindra, we made a careful note of it, in case we got lost. Since it was getting late, we decided not to go to the village that day. We drove along Lalpania Road, enjoying the clear path and admiring both Lugu Buru and the waters of the Tenughat Reservoir stretching below us.

The drive was extremely scenic and we took photos along the way, stopping the Alto here and there. I was of course disappointed to note that this beautiful landscape was a part of Bokaro district—and not Hazaribagh. 'Well, Bokaro people should also have *something* to see, I guess,' I consoled myself by patronizing my steel city neighbours. 'After all, once the flatland starts from here, it's all just that. They have a nice city, no doubt, but then, cities are everywhere, aren't they?'

Vinayak was full of obligatory *hmmms*.

At Lalpania, we saw a skinny waterfall. A stream originating from Lugu Buru flows down this fall into the flatland below. The monsoon had only just arrived in Jharkhand. Over the next few days, this waterfall wouldn't be skinny anymore.

'See this?' I pointed at the fall. 'It's good that they have this waterfall. They can turn it into a proper tourist place. Bokaro people are wealthier too, aren't they? It's so accessible—they could simply drive in with their cars.'

We drove through Lalpania and Kujju as the evening turned darker. From Kujju, we took the NH 33 back home.

On the third day, we drove straight to Pindra.

We turned towards the village from Lalpania Road, and after inquiring from the locals, reached the point where the cement road ended and the laterite path began. I parked the Alto near the last house of the village. An open land, called here a *tanr*, extended from one side of the car, dropping sharply into the river ahead. On the other side was the forest. I walked to the edge of the tanr, from where I saw the river.

The Bokaro had emerged from the shelter of the two massifs and acquired a considerable width. We had to follow it upstream and reach the place where the two mountains dropped into its bed. I asked a man coming along the laterite road if we could reach the river by taking the same path.

'*Haan, nadiye hai udhar*,' he said. There was only the river from there.

I had assumed that we would reach the river in a few quick minutes, but the road kept taking us deeper into the forest. Lugu Buru rose with us.

'You know there are *mamajis* here too,' I told Vinayak. 'We need to be a little careful.' The road didn't look like it would end anytime soon.

We also noticed it was an under-construction project. Trenches were dug up in places where bridges would be installed. It had rained the day before. The soil was wet and the road muddy. Instead of walking on the wet road, we were forced at many places to walk around it. At one time, we walked through a farmland. At another place, we had to be extremely cautious in the slippery mud. Puddles of various shapes and sizes had formed on the ground.

As we walked deeper, we realized that we had been walking for almost half an hour. The river was somewhere close, but because of the trees and bushes, we couldn't see it. Besides, there was no smooth way down to the water either. Each time we tried to leave the hill to reach the river, we encountered sharp falls. I began to wonder if we were lost.

Then, another man appeared on the road, carrying firewood on his shoulders. I was relieved. '*Nadi aage hai...?*' we asked him. '*Idhre hai nadiya.* Just across the forest,' he said. 'This way?' I repeated, pointing at an opening through the woods. He nodded confidently. We could go through that small gap between the trees.

It took us some time to find the correct path. When we entered through the gap, we found no trail to follow. We manoeuvred ourselves through the slippery, uneven land. There was a gully nearby, created by a monsoonal stream.

Like the waterfall at Lalpania, this stream too rushed down the precipices of Lugu Buru behind us. We stepped down that gully, grabbing branches, hunching under the canopies, cursing the irritating undergrowth. *Please, let there be no* mamaji. *Please, let there be no* mamaji. I repeated the sentence like a mantra in my head. Both Lugu Buru and Jhumra Pahad are sensitive areas. It was one thing to be alone in the forest, another to be with Vinayak. It was one thing to be kidnapped by *mamajis*, another to be held captive by the goddess of Lugu Buru.[20]

'You are also sometimes a worry only for me,' I had told him once. 'If I am alone, I know my responsibility is only towards me. If I fall, drown or die, it is still somewhat okay. With you, I have to be worried for you too. I can't even fall, drown or die—who will drive you back?'

Such thoughts formed in my head again as we stepped down the treacherous gully, but before I could worry any further, there it was—the river appeared before us.

Imagine blankness. Imagine two slanting lines, originating from the two top corners. They come down to join each other, but they do not meet. A white space keeps them apart.

Keep much of this whiteness intact but paint a thin streak of blue through it. The whiteness that remains, imagine it as sand. The blue is the water. The two lines that do not meet, imagine them as mountains. They are blue too, but theirs is a different shade, approaching green—not aqueous.

On both sides of the sand, put trees. Put so many trees that they proliferate across the lines, muddying the precision. In the whiteness above the sand, imagine clouds. Draw them softly and draw them voluminous. The sun hides behind them. Now and then, you find the light struggling to push through. The clouds release it in diffused beams.

Imagine sound, and give it to the water. This is your river. Water gurgles into itself. Imagine air, and give it to the sky. The wind sways from one mountain to the other. Meghdoot. The mountains talk about you. You, who have entered your own painting. You, who stand on the sand, a dwarf between two mountains. The river comes up to your feet.

Do not imagine birds because they will disturb the quiet, but imagine a foreboding, which the silence generates. This is the fear of trespassing, not only into another district but into a place that is too pure for humans. With this fear, imagine also the thrill. It creeps up your body. You look at the mountains and see light scattered upon their cloudy faces.

The plateau ends here, it also begins here. Like the river that originates in Hazaribagh but gives the city of Bokaro its name, the plateau too starts in Bokaro, and gives Hazaribagh its highland.

After crossing the water, I sat down on one of the sandy patches. Vinayak paced about the river, sometimes into the water and sometimes over the sand. I saw him searching for a rock to fix his phone on. 'Here, this spot is nice for a photo,' he said. We went to the spot and leaned against the boulder. Water circled past it, licking our shins.

Whenever the light hit the water, the river glimmered in silvery hues.

Between the mountains, we were two stick figures, flitting from one place to the other, weightless and irrelevant.

Epilogue

At one time, there was no Hazaribagh.

The land was just the plateau, and much of it was forest. Perhaps a few villages existed, far apart from each other. When the East India Company's cantonment came up in 1780–90, Hazaribagh, the town, followed soon afterwards. With the town came the sanatorium. Soldiers halted at Hazaribagh on their way to and from battles to rest and get better. This sanatorium was not a building. It was the perception of well-being which Hazaribagh stood for.

In 2017, twenty-six years old and battling depression, I returned to Hazaribagh from Delhi. Because Hazaribagh is my home, I often say that I can never *go* there. Instead, I can only and always *return*. So, I returned. But this time, I returned not to the hometown but the sanatorium.

Often, in books about travel, the movement happens from home to someplace else. The narrator leaves home to visit a different city or geography. With this book, the motion is reversed. Also in travel books, often the narrator recognizes in the end that the distance—between home and the destination—has spurred a change within them. The articulation of this change ends the tale, bringing the book to a close.

I will come to the changes later, but I want to note here some of my own distances.

The first, of course, was the distance between Delhi and Hazaribagh, between the cosmopolitan city and my small hometown. The second was the distance between the ordinary hometown and the vanishing sanatorium. This sanatorium had to resurrected. It had to be mapped, the boundaries had to be redrawn and its features had to be marked for my use.

All the places that occur in this book, and many others that exist outside of it, were ingredients in this recovery.

The pleasure of exploration brings with it the arrogance of discovery.

To detach pleasure from arrogance was a challenge.

While there were many places throughout my excursions, particularly waterfalls, that I 'found' on my own, it is also true that all these places had an apparent, if not documented, history of visitation. Even in the extreme depths of forest or escarpments, trails were always present. There were many people who had been to these places before.

In India, one finds villages and people in the most unexpected places. So, my explorations were hardly solitary. Nisanlagwa's axeman, Kurlungwa's Shukkar Oraon and the boy, Tiger, at Gittikocha Waterfall are reminders that stories are written by those who can write them—which is to say, by those who have had the kind of education that makes writing possible. This aspect is important in India, more so in Jharkhand, which remains one of the poorest states in the country. Earlier, I would say, 'Look, I have found these many waterfalls,' but gradually, the sentence changed to 'Look, I have gathered these many waterfalls.'

This change in verb helped replace the arrogance with fondness.

A crucial event I went through in Hazaribagh was to realize that while depression was a presence in my life, it could not be an end in itself.

In Delhi, it seemed like it was the only real thing. Moving past it felt impossible, which is why I had to leave the city. In Hazaribagh, I understood that there are ways to live with and beyond it.

It was this illness which had driven me further into the plateau, into the forest and along the rivers. There are many places in the book I wouldn't have gone to if I weren't pushed by something that was larger than myself.

Depression, people say, is a matter of the mind. I recall here the title of my friend Manjiri Indurkar's memoir, *It's All In Your Head, M*. Following this rhetoric, depression cannot be greater than oneself. But in reality, it *becomes*. And when it does, it extends way beyond the person who suffers from it. I left Delhi not because I hated the city, but because, at that time, I hated myself in it. I came to Hazaribagh because I thought I could love myself in it.

But how does one grow self-love out of self-hatred?

It is precisely here that the plateau intervened.

I loved it first. I loved its unrelenting flatness and I loved its swift rivers, its ruins and its forest. I loved its lakes and its reservoirs, and though the heat annoyed me, I loved its summers too. When this love spilled over, it became easier to gift some of it to myself.

I loved myself through the plateau.

If, in Delhi, the depression felt larger than me, in Hazaribagh, the plateau was greater than me. Against this greatness, the mind had to behave. So, I also changed, and this is the third kind of distance. Between what I was and what I am, between hatred and love, and cynicism and hope, is the plateau.

It contains me and my mind.

I finished the first draft of this book in April 2019.

Shortly afterwards, I went to Dumka and took up a teaching position for a year at a government college. At 250 kilometres from Hazaribagh, driving to Dumka meant driving through three landscapes of Jharkhand: the middle Chhotanagpur of Hazaribagh, the lower Chhotanagpur of Dhanbad and Jamtara, and the Rajmahal Hills of the Santhal Parganas.

Dumka was a low-altitude town, but there, I was surrounded by hills. This was because unlike Hazaribagh, Dumka was not on top of a plateau; instead, many hills and many smaller plateaus circled it. I took easily to Dumka's landscape, and there too I gathered many hills, rivers and ruins. But Dumka was also about people: shopkeepers who knew me as '*chhote* professor', students who nursed me whenever I fell ill, and friends who stayed late into the night with me as we studied, cooked, and sang karaoke.

I used to say that I like Delhi for the people, because my friends lived there, and Hazaribagh for the land. In Dumka, these two poles came together. I liked Dumka for the people *in* the land. This fondness wouldn't have appeared if I myself were starved of love in the first place.

Between the time I wrote this book and its publication, I travelled outwards from Hazaribagh into the larger Chhotanagpur Plateau.

I went to the forest of Palamau Tiger Reserve and walked along North Koel and Burha rivers. I watched Burha as it travelled from Chhattisgarh and fell down a high escarpment into Jharkhand, making the spectacular Lodh Waterfalls. I drove on the ghat roads of Netarhat to reach the Chhotanagpur's highest point and photographed constellations in the night from Koel View, shivering. I went to the quiet valley of Rajadera and strolled through the rows of pine trees that were once planted by the British along Sankh River. There, in the sparsely populated valley, I saw the ruins of a solitary bungalow, built lovingly by a romantic forest officer, once upon a time. Following the river further into the forest, I arrived at Sadnighagh, one of the most wondrous and obscure waterfalls in Jharkhand.

I went to Saranda too, and there, I saw how the Chhotanagpur ended in hilly fissures. Saranda is 'the land of seven hundred hills', and I watched at least a hundred of them from the high mining township of Kiriburu. From Kiriburu, I also looked down into the hazy valley below, on the south, and spotted miniscule homes and buildings of Barbil, Odisha, shimmering. I drove from Kiriburu to Chaibasa and found the earth red with iron mines.

In the end, life came a full circle.

I left Dumka after completing my one-year term at the college to prepare for doctoral studies. In the past few years, my experiences of travelling across the Chhotanagpur Plateau had instilled in me the desire to study the region and the narratives emerging from it more closely. As I started working on my proposal which I would later send to various universities, I saw the Chhotanagpur transform from an area of travel to an area of research.

In February 2021, I joined the Indian Institute of Technology, Delhi, as a research scholar. Here, I hope to reconcile Delhi with my past self, while diving deeper into Hazaribagh and the Chhotanagpur.

Notes

1. Bulu Imam has written an essay on the Old Benaras Road. Another often-mentioned road is the New Military Road. The latter was the repaired portion of the Old Benaras Road from Chas to Hazaribagh, which came up after the Ramgarh Battalion was stationed at Hazaribagh. Imam's essay appears in his book *Antiquarian Remains of Jharkhand* (INTACH and Aryan Books International, 2014). I consider *Antiquarian Remains of Jharkhand* as the most exhaustive work on the archaeological heritage of Hazaribagh.
2. The early history of Hazaribagh is recorded comprehensively by PC Roy Choudhury in *Hazaribagh Old Records (1761–1878)*. It was published in 1957, along with Roy Choudhury's *Hazaribagh Gazetteer*.
3. The gardens of Hazaribagh were mostly private gardens maintained inside the compounds of military and administrative officers. Bradley-Birt, on page 255 of *Chota Nagpore* described Hazaribagh thus: 'The town itself is almost hidden in its garden of trees.

Every compound has its share of sal and nim, karanj and tamarind, and every road is an avenue.'

The *Statistical, Sanitary and Medical Reports for the Year 1862*, published by the Army Medical Department and submitted to the British parliament observed:

> At Seetagurrah, about four miles east of the cantonment, a coffee and tea plantation is established; the coffee seems not to meet the expectation of the growers, but the tea does very well. Cotton has also been recently tried; the expectation of its success is held, but it is too soon to form a definite opinion. In the private gardens in the station, as well as at Seetagurrah, every description almost of English vegetables is produced, cabbages, peas, beans, onions, lettuces, celery, radishes, with potatoes, carrots, turnips, etc.; and with proper care everything of this kind required for European troops could be cheaply provided. Many of the European and Caubul flowers and fruits that will not grow in many other parts of India thrive admirably in the gardens of Hazareebaugh.

4. G Hunter Thompson's *A Geographical, Statistical & General Report on the District of Hazareebaugh, Surveyed During Seasons 1858–59 to 1862–63* is available on Google Play Books. Thompson recommends Hazaribagh Plateau as a potential site for the new capital of India on page 3.
5. Edward Money's *The Cultivation and Manufacture of Tea* (1870) lists Hazaribagh as one of the eleven

'tea districts' in India on page 13. However, Money didn't find Hazaribagh's climate favourable for good produce. On page 24, he remarks:

> This district I have resided in since I wrote the first edition of this Essay. The climate is too dry, and hot winds are felt there. A great compensation, though, is labour; it is more abundant and cheaper in this district than in any other. The carriage is all by land, and it is some distance to the rail. But the Tea gardens at Hazareebaugh can never vie with those in Eastern Bengal, in as much as the climate is very inferior. The soil is very poor.

On page 62 of *Accounts and Papers of the House of Commons* (vol. 48), published in 1874, Lieutenant-Colonel H.M. Boddam, then the Deputy Commissioner of Hazaribagh, mentions three tea plantations in his 1872 report to Colonel E.T. Dalton, then the Commissioner of the Chota Nagpur Division. These three plantations were established at Sitagarha Hill, Mahudi Hill and Jhumra Hill. *Accounts and Papers of the House of Commons* (vol. 48) is available on Google Books and may be pursued for statistics on tea cultivation in Hazaribagh.

6. Juljul was recorded as 'Mount Gloomy' by Captain Robert Smith in his 1813 sketches 'Mount Gloomy and New Road near Hazaribagh' and 'Monuments and Mount Gloomy'. The two sketches can be viewed online on the British Library's website.
7. For Hazaribagh as a sanatorium, see the extract below.

It appears on page 297 of the *Statistical, Sanitary and Medical Reports for the Year 1862*, published by the Army Medical Department (see also note 3).

> Documentary evidence of Medical Officers as to the experience of the healthiness of Hazareebaugh is only obtainable for this Report from 1859 to the present time; but for that period it is unanimous and forcibly expressive in favour of the station as a residence for Europeans. Surgeon Holton, of the 77th Regiment, says in his Report for 1861: "On the arrival of the regiment at Hazareebaugh, the men were in a very weakly state, even those men at duty were greatly debilitated." In his Report for 1862 he observes, "the climate of Hazareebaugh is changeable but cooler than the plains; April and May are really the only hot months and these are generally tempered by the occurrence of thunder storms with rain and hail. I consider the climate well suited for Europeans, and conducive to health, and would exercise a very beneficial effect on constitutions weakened by a residence in the plains, as proved by the wonderful change in the health of the men of the 77th Regiment." Again he observes, "In fact I look upon it as a sanitarium. In support of this statement I wish to mention that when called upon in the beginning of the year to select men for the sanitarium at Darjeeling, I felt averse to send any there from the experience I had already of the benefit derived by the regiment from the year

> spent at Hazareebaugh. However, I selected a few men most likely to be benefited by the change and sent them, keeping back others in much the same condition and I have no hesitation in stating that on the arrival of some of these men from Darjeeling a few days ago, they were not in as good condition as the men who were kept at Hazareebaugh."

FB Bradley-Birt, on pages 259-260 in his book *Chota Nagpore* (1903), brings up Hazaribagh against Darjeeling too:

> Hazaribagh owes much to Sir George Campbell, a Lieutenant-Governor of thirty years ago. He visited the station twice, spending portions of the hot weather there and contemplating making it the Government resort, instead of Darjeeling, during the summer months and rains.

8. The letters pertaining to the construction of sanatoriums on Juljul and Parasnath Hills appear on pages 153-58 and page 163 in Roy Choudhury's *Hazaribagh Old Records (1761–1878).*
9. Vishvendu Jaipuriar's May 22, 2012 news report 'Citizen Saviours for Hazaribagh Lakes' in *The Telegraph* highlights the connection between the tribal uprisings of the 1830s and the construction of the jail by Captain Thomas Wilkinson.
10. Roy Choudhury mentions on page 66 of *Hazaribagh Old Records (1761–1878)* that the present Central Jail is the larger extension of the former Agency Jail which could initially house a total of 164 convicts.

11. The circumstances resulting in the construction of the European Penitentiary and the enterprise's relationship with racial hierarchy is elucidated by Harald Fischer-Tine in his essay 'Hierarchies of Punishment in Colonial India: European Convicts and the Racial Dividend, c. 1860-1890'. The essay appears in the anthology *Empires and Boundaries: Race, Class and Gender in Colonial Settings* (2009), edited by Harald Fischer-Tine and Susanne Gehrmann, and published by Routledge.
12. For Chevers' observations on the site for the new penitentiary, see his 1862 'Memorandum on the Hazaribagh Jail', reproduced verbatim by Roy Choudhury on page 68 of *Hazaribagh Old Records (1761-1878)*.
13. Dr John Martin Coates appears on page 162 in Eyre Chatterton's *The Story of Fifty Years' Mission Work in Chhota Nagpur* (1901):

    > A clever civil surgeon, Surgeon-Col. Coates, when resident there, by carefully utilizing some streams, succeeded in giving to the station two extremely pretty lakes, which added considerably to its beauty.

    On the same page, Chatterton also explains the difference between Hazaribagh town and Hazaribagh 'station':

    > The term "station" in India is applied to the settlement where European officials and military people reside. Hazaribagh town and "station" lie

at an elevation of nearly two thousand feet above sea-level on the northern Chhota Nagpur plateau, which extends in a pretty park-like country, well cultivated, for many miles around.

14. The conversion of the European Penitentiary into a boys' reformatory is also highlighted by FB Bradley-Birt in *Chota Nagpore* on pages 255-58.
15. Bulu Imam has documented several rock-art sites occurring along the length of Karanpura Valley. His private museum 'Sanskriti' at Dipugarha in Hazaribagh town has a replica of the Isko rock art painted over the length of a wall.
16. A fine overview of Hazaribagh is provided by Sir John Wardle Houlton in *Bihar: The Heart of India* (1949). I have mentioned Houlton in chapter two, in the context of Canary Hill, but his comment on Barkagaon, or the larger Karanpura Valley, on page 154 of his book, has been prophetic:

    This is at present a fertile rice-growing valley; but it is in the coal-belt, and will no doubt be transformed in time by the expansion of industry.

17. Subhashis Das' *The Archaeoastronomy of a Few Megalithic Sites of Jharkhand* (Niyogi Books, 2017) offers a detailed explanation of the Pankri Barwadih Megalithic Complex in Barkagaon. Das has documented several more megalithic sites in and around Hazaribagh.
18. As of April 2021, the 'Creepy Road' from Rajhar to

Motra is seen repaired and converted to a single-lane, tarmac road.

19. The lore of cows and bulls falling from waterfalls repeats in two places in Hazaribagh. The first is at Baratpichharwa on Bokaro River near Sarbaha village and the second is at Amandhara-Bailgiri on Rajhar Nala near Kurlungwa and Rajhar villages. Amandhara-Bailgiri Waterfall is paired with the Gittikocha Waterfall downstream. The proposed Motra Coal Mine Project has made these two waterfalls' future uncertain.
20. HD Christian's article 'Some Stories Current in Hazaribagh Regarding Lugu Baba' documents a few myths and legends associated with Lugu Buru. In a couple of these stories, teleportation of people is a major event. The article was published in *Journal of the Bihar and Orissa Research Society* (vol. 7) in March 1921, pages 57-59.

Acknowledgements

I thank my editor Kartikeya Jain at Speaking Tiger Books.

I also thank Shreya Gupta and Radhika Shenoy for their observations on the manuscript. I thank the publisher Ravi Singh for his trust in my book. I thank my agent Kanishka Gupta for steering me towards prose.

I thank my historians in Hazaribagh, notably Mr Bulu Imam and Mr Subhashis Das. I thank my brother Siddharth Pandey for encouraging me to articulate my appreciation for the plateau landscape. I thank Siddharth also for introducing me to the works of Robert Macfarlane, Nan Shepherd and Edward Abbey.

I thank Ayesha Mallik and Debabrata Sen at Gibraltar, Canary Hill Road, Hazaribagh for telling me about their home's history and allowing me to photograph it for my archives.

I thank my companions in the book: Raza Kazmi, Shubhodeep Datta, Rahul Kumar, Aditya Mandal, Vinayak Bhatt, Mirtunjay Sharma and Sujit Prasad. Though he does not appear in the book, I thank my friend Reyan Najmi for accompanying me to Jhumra Pahad in December 2020. I thank my relatives from Muzaffarpur. I thank my uncle Sameer Mishra and his family in Hazaribagh who travelled with me to Amandhara-Bailgiri Waterfall near Rajhar. I thank my guides: Shukkar Oraon, Md. Danish Ansari, and 'Axeman'.

I thank the Hazaribagh District Administration.

I thank Mr Ravi Shankar Shukla, formerly the Deputy Commissioner of Hazaribagh, Mr Dileep Yadav, formerly the Divisional Forest Officer (Wildlife Range), and Mr Anand, formerly the District Public Relations Officer, for their assistance and many conversations. I thank my friends Shubhodeep Datta, Pretty Priyadarshini and Charu Madan, who at the time of writing this book, were working with the administration in various capacities.

I thank Raza Kazmi and Siddharth Pandey again for being my first readers. I thank Dr Rajesh Kumar at Vinoba Bhave University, Hazaribagh, and Dr Achyut Chetan at St Xavier's University, Kolkata, for being my first readers. I thank my friends Raghav Mani and Kanchan Maji for keeping me alive in Dumka. I thank my students and colleagues at both Santal Parganas College and the Postgraduate Department of English, Sido Kanhu Murmu University, Dumka, for their love during editing of this book.

I thank my friends at Think Inc Studio, Delhi, and Sampark Foundation, Noida.

I thank Mr Richard Alford, former Secretary of the Charles Wallace India Trust, and Dr Gemma Robinson at the

University of Stirling, UK, for selecting me as their 2014-15 Charles Wallace Fellow. I thank Dr Mary Brooks at the University of Durham, UK, for inviting me every year to talk with her students about Hazaribagh's heritage. I thank Mr James Rattray at Killiecrankie, Scotland, for a most unique friendship.

I thank editors Aditya Mani Jha and Vaishna Roy for encouraging me to write about Hazaribagh. The articles they published in *The Hindu Businessline* and *The Hindu Sunday Magazine*, respectively, served as testing grounds for both myself and this book.

I thank my friends Arjun Rajendran, Nandini Dhar, Manjiri Indurkar and Tanuj Solanki for no particular reason but to say that I love them and I miss them. I thank Arpita Sarker, Sanchi Budhiraja and Shyamalima Kalita for their enduring friendship. I thank Geetika Sinha for trusting me more than I trust myself. I thank my friend Aman Singh for his love and good wishes.

Finally, I thank my parents for gifting me the plateau.